SAMUEL LEEDS'
SUCCESS
STUDENTS

SAMUEL LEEDS'

SUCCESS

STUDENTS

(Volume 1)

Thirty inspirational Property Investors' case studies packed with hot tips from students who have one thing in common – they're all 'smashing it' as property investors!

Introduction

Every week Samuel Leeds transforms people's lives by empowering them to become financially free through property investing.

This has been his all-consuming mission since launching Property Investors – the biggest training company of its kind in the UK.

Before the pandemic the free Property Investors Crash Course was held regularly at major venues in London and Birmingham, with 500-1,000 people from an average of 17 countries flocking to each event. The silver lining in the Covid crisis was the launch of Property Investors' online crash course and *Samuel 365*, an unrivalled comprehensive package of training and support. (Visit www.property-investors.co.uk for more information).

Our students come from a host of different cultures and all walks of life. Many of them are looking for a way out of a job they hate, sick of working nine-to-five with limited holidays. They recoil at the thought of being chained to their desks for the next 40 years with only a meagre pension to look forward to.

Others are just starting out, often with little or even no money to invest. They are all driven by a hunger to succeed and the desire to make life better for themselves and their families. Some of the men and women, who enrol on the crash course and opt for advanced training, have capital to invest but lack the knowledge and skills to achieve an automatic income through property

No matter what their background, all the participants crave freedom and want to be in complete control of their lives, spending every day doing exactly what they choose to do. They know that the right education can open up new horizons and are ready to take that first, vital step of attending one of the regular two-day crash courses.

The success of Property Investors is down to the phenomenal success of its students. They are walking proof of the value of the teachings. A large number of individuals have become financially free after absorbing the training – and more join their ranks each week.

The investors in this volume have all appeared on Samuel Leeds' popular YouTube show, *Winners on a Wednesday,* talking about their journey and how they have been helped by Property Investors. The following chapters contain precious tips and examples of how they have each capitalised on what they have learned. Their successes offer inspiration and hope to others embarking on property ventures.

All the students have benefited greatly from Samuel Leeds' encyclopaedic knowledge, so that they no longer have to work long hours to cover their bills. They have made their families proud by becoming financially independent – just like Samuel did as a teenager.

The definition of financial freedom differs greatly from person to person. For some £2,000-£3,000 a month might be enough to meet their outgoings and leave enough over to enjoy life. For others the figure could be far higher.

Samuel first glimpsed what the term meant to him when he was just 24 and already a property millionaire. He was on honeymoon in Croatia with his bride Amanda, when he realised they could carry on island hopping forever and just live off the revenue from his string of properties.

However, as a born entrepreneur with an eagle eye for a golden opportunity, just sitting back doing nothing was never going to be his lifestyle choice. His overriding sense of purpose has since propelled him to even greater heights.

Still only 30, the self-made multi-millionaire has completed hundreds of lucrative property deals. He also owns Ribbesford House, a Grade II listed country mansion in Worcestershire, once used by General de Gaulle to train Free French cadets in readiness for the D-Day landings during WWII.

Samuel's strong faith has also been a major driving force in his desire to help other people to follow in his footsteps. As a committed Christian, the father-of-three believes that the pursuit of wealth is a force for good, especially when used to benefit others. As a keen philanthropist he is well known for his charity work, financing fresh water projects in remote African villages and helping to rebuild schools in the poorest areas of Uganda. In addition, he contributes to many other worthy causes closer to home.

He left school at 16 and, despite having no money, Samuel bought his first buy-to-let at below market value shortly before his 18th birthday. He was too young to apply for a mortgage but got permission to put the house in his stepfather's name. After refinancing the terraced house up to its true value, he paid off the bridging loan, pocketing a monthly profit of £950 in rent.

That modest home in Bournville, Birmingham, ignited a multi-million pound business. By the time Samuel was 19, his passive income from rents dwarfed the average person's salary. He realised early in life that property investing can be the key to financial independence and could have retired in his early twenties.

His investment strategies rely solely on knowledge and formulas, not feelings or luck. Every single property in his portfolio, from his first buy-to-let to his grand country estate, was the result of the methodical methods he now teaches.

He maintains, however, that the best investment he ever made was in himself. Even as a 17-year old he had an unquenchable thirst for knowledge. Wearing an ill-fitting £30 suit from Asda, he attended specialist property networking events, constantly rubbing shoulders with successful business people. In 2014, as chairman of Property Investors, Samuel held his inaugural two-day crash course. The first student to enrol was Jael Spooner who, inspired by his teachings, went on to buy her council flat in London and open a late night bar in the City with 20 staff and a £1m turnover.

Jael's story is the first to be featured in this book about students whose lives have been changed by Property Investors. They were all fired by Samuel's enthusiasm for his subject and inspired to carve out their own niche in the industry.

Many of the featured students progressed enormously within a short space of time. Andrea Harber, for example, took just two years to build up a portfolio of seven properties generating thousands of pounds a month. Another hugely successful trainee was Alasdair Cunningham who now works closely with Samuel Leeds. Within two years of going into business, Alasdair was earning more than £30,000 a month from sourcing property deals for investors and renting out accommodation.

John Raybould, who joined Property Investors Academy, became financially free before finishing his full-time university course. Former Royal Marine Joe Lane had to learn to talk and walk again after an horrific skiing accident. He fought back to become a property entrepreneur, having trained with the academy, and now makes a good living from his investments.

This is the first volume of an ongoing series of success stories reflecting an ever increasing army of entrepreneurs becoming financially free through Samuel Leeds' training.

The publication of this book coincides with Samuel's 30th birthday and aptly consists of 30 chapters, each dedicated to a different student.

Contents

Chapter 1 – Jael Spooner

From being on benefits to running a London bar, Samuel Leeds' first student is living the dream

One-time model and waitress Jael Spooner has the distinction of being the first student to enrol on Samuel Leeds' Property Investors Crash Course in 2014.

Inspired by Samuel's story and his teachings, Jael went on to buy her council flat in London and opened a late-night bar in the city, raising £250,000 with her partner to fund the venture.

The 31-year-old describes the club, called Tunnel London, as the best Afrobeat venue in the UK, with 20 staff, a turnover of about £1 million a year and a net profit of 15 per cent.

Jael also lets out a flat in Kentish Town under a rent-to-rent arrangement which brings her in a further £1,000 a month. As part of the agreement, she pays the owner, who lives abroad, a guaranteed monthly rent and then re-lets the accommodation at a higher rate. She found her tenants in just half an hour.

She has also helped friends fund improvements to their homes on the condition that she is allowed to 'double her money' by renting out their spare rooms.

For Jael it has been a remarkable journey. She was brought up in west London after coming to this country, where her grandparents were born, when she was eight, having travelled extensively in Africa. Her home was a council flat, which Jael shared with her mother, brothers and sisters but at 16 she moved out because she wanted her own space. She stayed in a succession of hostels all over the capital, living on benefits, until her local authority found her a permanent place to stay.

"It was a lovely studio apartment and I fell in love with it. I said to my mum, when I was 18, I'm going to buy this flat. Years later I did. I bought it under the right to acquire scheme which enabled me to buy the property at a reduced price.

"I've just got planning permission to develop it. I will eventually put it on a buy-to-let mortgage and rent it out."

Despite her success, she remains ambitious to take her property investing to a new level and build up a passive income following the birth of her son. So early in 2020, she attended another Property Investors Crash Course to gain more knowledge.

The mother-of-one was immediately struck by the difference between the first crash course, when she learnt about the rent-to-rent strategy, and the second one.

"I remember there were about eight of us, including Samuel, in a room in Birmingham. We were circled around a laptop and he talked about how to become financially free. He was amazing. I didn't know it was his first one because he was really confident.

"It was such a beautiful experience when I went to the second crash course. I walked in and there were 1,000 people in a theatre with a massive screen and a phenomenal trainer telling people how to source properties. I was walking round saying I used to be here when there was eight of us. Look how big it's got!"

Jael signed up immediately for the company's academy which did not exist when she initially went on the crash course.

"I wrote on the academy paper I'm going to rock your world. It just felt right."

So far, she has completed 'Business of Property Investing,' one of the academy training programmes, and has also gone networking to increase her contacts.

Her goal is to build a property portfolio, take on more rent-to-rents and also lease option agreements.

"When I fell pregnant in 2019 everyone was saying you're in a good position now. You can sit back. You can train your staff and go in once in a while to retrain them – relax and enjoy the fruits of your labour. Whilst I was pregnant, I thought God forbid if anything happened to my business right now. How would we survive? Even though it sounds very romantic having a business I'm still looking for that cash flow."

Jael credits Samuel for playing a big part in introducing her to 'her career and dreams' and giving her the confidence to raise finance.

She is passionate about public speaking and is keen to join him on stage again soon, having already given an emotional talk about her property journey at a previous event.

"What taught me was training myself. I would always train my staff and tell them the story of my success. I started as a glass collector, worked as a waitress, then a head waitress, manager and a general manager. Then I had my own late-night bar. That inspires them to work hard because it's not what you do, it's how you do it."

Property Investors' chairman Samuel Leeds said: "Jael is one of the hungriest people I know, and she is a powerful, confident woman. She has worked so hard over the last six years. She should be so proud of what she's achieved."

JAEL'S TIPS

On networking: "Get out there, just talk to people and be open. Take notes. That really helped me reading them afterwards. Networking is good for building rapport with people in the industry. You can meet your whole power team through that. It's great as well to immerse yourself with like-minded people because you are the company you keep."

On raising finance: "To raise finance you have to paint a picture for people that will enable them to visualise what it is you're talking about, even though it's not there. I had to take people into a venue that was just a dusty shell with no bar and convince potential investors that 300 people were going to walk through the door. I showed them where the bar and tables would be, and the VIP area, and had to persuade them. They had to see it, live it and feel it. Once they did, the money came."

"Life throws so many different challenges at you, so you have to be able to truly believe what you're doing is the right thing. You have to not care what other people think. That's the biggest thing I'd want a lot of women to know, especially in this time when we really care about the 'likes' and what people say on social media. What builds confidence is not caring what other people think and just being yourself."

"I always tell people that I am a property entrepreneur. It led to me getting my rent-to-rent in Kentish Town. I invested a little bit of money in doing it up and rented the three rooms out on the same day I got it."

"Make sure you buy all Samuel's books. That will give you confidence when you're in the crash course to then go on to the academy because you think I already know a lot so now I can go to that next level. I bought them all and gave myself the best chance to succeed."

"I have every reason not to be where I am today. I lived in a council flat in west London. Why I am in this position and why I am going to go further is because I'm surrounding myself with the right people – the people I want to be like. That's what the crash course and academy give you."

Chapter 2 – Joe Lane

Former Royal Marine battles back from a serious injury to become a 'hot shot' property investor

Former Royal Marine Joe Lane, from Wareham in Dorset, had to relearn to talk and walk after an horrific skiing accident, but fought back to become a property entrepreneur.

Six years on and the ex-captain and troop commander in the elite Royal Marines fighting force is already earning enough money to be financially free.

He was in a coma for three days and also lost his hearing temporarily, but heroically battled his way back to a full recovery, despite doctors' fears he could be left in a permanent vegetative state.

Now the veteran of the war in Afghanistan has forged a new career, snapping up houses at below market value, doing them up and then renting them out.

True to his training, Joe who attended Poole Grammar School, has proved himself adaptable to any circumstance. He has a passive income of more than £2,000 which covers all his monthly expenses.

The 36-year-old, however, refuses to rest on his laurels and is trying to build up a property portfolio that will create long-term wealth for his family, including his wife Laura and their children.

"I was never just going to sit at home and twiddle my thumbs," said Joe who served with the Royal Marines for eight and a half years.

Three days after the young officer passed out, he flew to Afghanistan in 2008, where he took part in helicopter assaults and regularly came under fire. His troop also carried out reconnaissance work for the Americans and located a bomb factory.

On another occasion he witnessed a suicide bomber blow himself up. The explosion took out a compound but fortunately no-one else was hurt.

"We also flew into a hornet's nest in Marjah. Literally the minute we hit the ground there were bullets flying around everywhere. My men were lucky. None of us were killed, although two guys from a friend's troop were injured after they were shot."

Joe was also despatched to post-war Iraq, where he set up armoured vehicle convoys to avoid improvised explosive devices, and escort people across the border into Kuwait.

Having survived all these dangers, Joe was seriously injured while on a skiing holiday in St Anton am Arlberg in the Austrian Alps.

"I was going down a black run in a bit of a whiteout. I don't really remember what happened, but I must have hit a lip, gone over and smashed my head on the ice. I woke up three days later in hospital in Innsbruck. I couldn't walk or talk. I'd lacerated the part of the brain that operates all your muscular movement. The cut was within a third of a millimetre of the bit that controls your breathing and heart rate, so it was quite a close call."

After being transferred back to the UK, he spent six months at two rehabilitation centres for injured forces personnel. In total, it took him 18 months to learn how to walk and talk again.

He spent some time setting up a shop to raise money for injured Marines and their families. Then a friend suggested he attend a property investing event in Plymouth. The speaker was Samuel Leeds.

Joe already owned a single-let house in Poole but wanted to progress to the next level. So he enrolled in Samuel Leeds' Property Investors Academy. Over a period of a year, he attended a range of advanced courses with specialist coaches. He also had a one-to-one session with Samuel where he presented a business plan and got feedback.

As well as the two-day crash course, Joe attended the *Deal Finding Extravaganza* and *Never Use Your Own Money Again* seminars as part of his training.

It gave him the skills and knowledge he needed to find good deals and properties he could buy without necessarily putting down any of his own money.

He bought his first house in Derby for £96,500 in 2016. After spending £15,000 on a new boiler and redecorating the house, it is now worth £120,000. All four rooms are constantly rented, yielding £1,400 a month which Joe works out is a return on investment of about 25 per cent.

At the same time, he bought a multi-let flat in Plymouth and then added another house in Nottingham to his portfolio. He got it at auction for £98,000 in a joint venture with a friend.

"I managed to get four investors on board who lent us just under £120,000. It was acquired under a scheme called Buy, Refurbish, Refinance, Rent. We're planning to refinance it with a mortgage for £165,000, which is what I believe it will be worth when it's done up. Hopefully we'll leave no money in and rent it out for between £600 and £700 a month."

The investors, who are all ex-work colleagues, agreed to lend their money for up to six months on a return basis of between 5 and 8 per cent. If they want their money back then, the refinancing deal will enable him to repay the loan. But he is hoping he can persuade them to reinvest in another project.

Joe has also put in another offer on a house in Sunderland which he is planning to turn into a multi-let with up to four tenants.

"I won't be able to get a mortgage because the offer is below £50,000 but it's just opposite the hospital, so it should give me a high return on investment.

"Finding below market value properties is the secret to success. Derby and Nottingham are both really good for capital appreciation and house prices in the North East are fantastic."

It is manageable having property in the north, he says. On one occasion, he flew to Sunderland from Bristol Airport. "It was only an hour on the plane. Then I got a hire car and went property hunting. I met up with Laura's sister for coffee in the afternoon and saw a few more properties. Afterwards I met up with a good agent who deals with houses of multiple occupation."

Looking to the future, he intends to move into offering serviced accommodation for short lets through his company, Top Hat Property.

Joe, who now lives in Long Ashton near Bristol, is already enjoying the freedom his passive earnings give him. He took two months off in Italy at the start of his property journey and in the summer cycled across the Pyrenees from Biarritz to Barcelona with his dad, two brothers and the godfather of his one-year-old daughter, Hattie.

"The crash course was totally eye-opening and entertaining. I had an amazing weekend and it changed my life. The academy has also been very important to me. I've been able to surround myself with like-minded people and talk to them," he added.

Samuel said: "Joe has been very successful in implementing the knowledge he has acquired through our training programmes and is reaping the benefits of his hard work. He has not only been a great student – he's a great guy too. I think he'll go far."

JOE'S TIPS

"One of the biggest lessons I've learnt is to put your story out there. Let people know what you do. Put it over in a concrete way so people are happy and confident in what you can achieve for them."

"I also believe it's good to look at different strategies but have a clear focus about what type of property investor you want to be."

"Don't ever take shortcuts either when you're doing a refurbishment because that will come back and bite you in the bottom."

"When searching for a tenant to fill an empty room, it's tempting to put the first one that comes along in there but if that person's not right that will cause you an absolute nightmare down the line.

"When you're dealing with an investor, always do what you say you're going to do. Be trustworthy and be yourself."

Chapter 3 – Andrea Harber

Estate agent learns that renting the house she lives in makes sense when becoming a property investor

Estate agent Andrea Harber decided to sell her house and move into a rented house with her family to release funds for property investing after being diagnosed with breast cancer.

Andrea latched onto the idea after attending a Property Investors' Crash Course run by Samuel Leeds during which he spoke about the benefits of renting where you live.

Two years later she is in remission from the cancer and financially free with a portfolio of seven properties. It includes a block of flats and a house being converted into a seven-bed HMO, earning her a monthly profit of £4,200. Once the latter is up and running the mother-of-three expects her income to rise to about £8,000 a month after all her costs are paid.

Andrea enrolled on the crash course in September 2017 after seeing Samuel on the BBC documentary *Meet the Landlords* and being impressed by his enthusiasm.

'When Samuel talked on the course about how he rents where he lives, I thought it sounded crazy, so I asked him during a break exactly why he did this. He replied why would he want to put a huge deposit down on a barn if he could invest that money into something else. It gave him flexibility.

'That sowed a seed in my mind that it was a really good idea and I spent the rest of the break looking at houses I could rent which were nicer than where we lived.'

A few months later, however, came the devastating blow that she had breast cancer which led to her having an operation in May 2018 and then treatment in Mexico in the same year.

'It put everything on hold but at the same time it gave me a kick. I thought I really need to go for this because you don't know how long you've got on this earth. If you want to do something you need to go for it.'

She and her husband Spencer, a police officer, decided to put their house up for sale and then went together to another Property Investors Crash Course for him to learn more.

Andrea subsequently signed up for the three-day *Deal Finding Extravaganza* which she attended in between hospital visits.

The couple had already done some property investing previously, owning three rental houses, one in Slough and two in High Wycombe in Buckinghamshire where they live.

They had also bought a buy-to-let in Wolverhampton before going to the crash course.

'I learnt so much on those three days of advanced training. It was a lot more in depth than the crash course. I learnt from it that the house we'd bought in Wolverhampton was not a great house and there's lot more to property investing than just buying a house and renting it out. We've now sold it.'

Andrea also watched Samuel's YouTube videos, listened to his podcasts, read his books and immersed herself in the subject before setting up her own limited company, Harber Homes.

The first property she bought after selling their home to move into rented accommodation was in High Wycombe. It was a rundown two-bedroom house for sale below market value. She paid £202,000 and spent £22,000 on renovating it. The property is now valued at £285,000 and she has pulled out £200,000 after refinancing it.

The 44-year-old says she has excellent tenants who pay her a monthly rent of £1,175. Her interest-only mortgage payments amount to £487 a month, giving her a good profit margin, even after maintenance costs.

'Funnily enough the estate agency I work for sold the house next door but one for £287,000 a few months earlier, so I knew the price was good.'

After that Andrea bought a seven-bed HMO near where she lives, using a relative's money for the deposit. The mortgage payments are met by her and they split the profits from the rent equally.

'He had money to invest but no idea about property. I put the idea to him. I said this house will earn this much. It was all done legally through a solicitor.'

Her next purchase was the house in Lane End, also in Buckinghamshire, which she is in the throes of turning into another seven-bed HMO. Again, she bought it below market value.

'Houses in that road sell for about £325,000. I got it for £260,000 because it was being sold through the council. As it was a cash sale, I was able to secure it at that price. The same investor is putting all the money in. I'm paying for the refurbishment. We'll split the profits 50-50. He's got the first legal charge on the house which means he has first call on any funds available from the sale of the property. It was done through solicitors again.'

Some of the money she made from her first deal will finance a double side extension to the house to provide seven rooms and six bathrooms. Once that work is finished, she will again refinance it and take out funds for her next project.

'I give my investor a statement each month on what the expenditure has been on the properties and what he gets. I want to be transparent, so if something's gone wrong in a month he can see that's why he's got less money.'

Her fourth deal saw her acquire a block of seven flats in Blackpool. She plans to run three of them as serviced accommodation for short stays. The other flats are rented already. She has an 'excellent' management agent who has helped her organise the refurbishment work. He also rents out furnished accommodation in Blackpool and offers a bespoke service setting up rooms in a boutique style.

Andrea got a bargain once more. The owner had bought the apartments in 2011 for £210,000 and refurbished the whole building including rewiring it. She negotiated a price of £183,000. Her investment amounted to £55,000.

'The mortgage payments on that are peanuts. I will make a profit of probably £3,600-3,700 a month. That's a conservative estimate. I worked out the figures on a 15-night occupancy rate for the serviced accommodation.'

It has not all been easy. Due to the commercial nature of the sale it took a year to complete before it finally went through in November 2019. She has also had some issues with tenants and three boilers breaking down in one year but has weathered these problems with a determination to keep going.

'I've had other setbacks with friends who were diagnosed at the same time as me dying. That can be quite difficult because you just think, is it going to happen to me? You've always got that worry. It's just made me go for what I'm doing and learn as much as I can.

'My family thought we were mad renting where we live but it's not like I don't own any properties. I just happen to be renting the one where I'm living.'

Andrea chooses to work part-time for an estate agency in High Wycombe because she says she loves meeting people and advising clients.

'I try to guide people, say if they've inherited some money, not just to buy one house but to spread out the investment. If people are looking for an HMO, they tend to send me out because I can advise on the management aspect of it and the licensing required. My knowledge is probably greater than just someone showing them round the house.

'One man I advised has bought two properties and set up a limited company. It's nice to be able to help and give something back.'

Samuel Leeds has a personal reason to be grateful to her as she found the perfect rented house for him in Beaconsfield with its fast links to London and good schools. It was under budget too.

He said: 'She's had a tough time healthwise, and on the property side, but actually what she's achieved has been amazing. The return on investment on the Blackpool flats is just incredible. You could easily invest £55,000 in a single let house that's going to make you £300 a month as opposed to well over ten times that amount which is what Andrea is forecasting. That deal alone would make someone financially free.'

Andrea has been on many crash courses and other Property Investors training programmes since to soak up as much knowledge as possible. She even took her eight-year-old daughter Bella to one crash course and she has now been bitten by the property bug.

Her mother often takes her on viewings as well, and she has read Samuel's *Buy Low Rent High Book*.

'She doesn't like some of the houses I take her to. Sometimes I pretend we're going to live there, and she says mummy, I don't want to live in this house. As Samuel says, it's not about buying a pretty house. It's the ugly houses that make the most money.'

ANDREA'S TIPS

"The three most valuable things I learnt on the course and the advanced training was firstly, rent where you live because selling your house gives you lots of cash to invest in property. It was an epiphany moment for me when Samuel talked about that on the crash course.

"Secondly, it gave me the confidence to successfully joint venture with people and thirdly, it taught me to find the good deals. It gives you an overall awareness of what's good and what's not. On the crash course you learn about getting a good return on investment on properties."

"Read *Buy Low Rent High* and as many books as you can about property. Listen to podcasts as well and subscribe to Samuel's YouTube channel. There's so much free content on there with great advice."

Chapter 4 – Josh Knecht

Property entrepreneur who started out living in a shed eyes up £100,000 Ferrari

When Josh Knecht started life as a property entrepreneur, nobody knew he was living in a shed next to a trainline.

Now less than ten years later the 30-year-old, from Woking, is on course to realise his dream of owning a £100,000 Ferrari. Along the way he has raised more than £1m in private finance to create his wealth through a string of property deals.

Josh, who suffers from dyslexia, spent a winter sleeping in an outbuilding next to a train track in temperatures of minus 8C. He had used up all his money on looking after his sick parents who have since died.

By day, he went out to networking events persuading investors to lend him cash to buy houses, which he would either rent or do up and sell, in return for giving them a percentage of the profit.

He still had an old Ford Mondeo to get to meetings and no one suspected his plight, he said.

"I remember the shed was near Croydon. The owner was the only one who knew I was there, but it was a tough few months. I had nowhere else to go. The door didn't even shut properly. How I survived I don't know.

"I would go to my local boatyard because I could have a shower at six o clock before they opened up. I could then drop my stuff at the dry cleaners, pick up my new clothes, get changed and drive to property events. I'd say I'm doing property. If you want to come and have a coffee, let's talk about investments. I was offering good deals and no one ever realised what was going on in the background. If they had, they wouldn't have trusted me.

"I hadn't got my own cash flow at the time because of the situation with my parents. They were living in rented accommodation after they lost most of their money on bad investments.

"Thankfully living in the shed turned out to be a temporary thing and it was quite a long time ago, but it was like I'm never ever going back to that point. That gives you masses of drive."

Josh says he learnt as an eight-year-old there was money to be made from bricks and mortar. His father was a successful window salesman who lived with his family in a £1m house in Woking. At the back was an annexe which they rented out for £700 a month.

"The rent would literally come in cash in the back door and would go into a drawer under the phone before it went to the bank. I would look at all the rolls of cash. That was enough to tell me that if you bought property, and rented it out, you'd make money. That excited me."

Josh also learnt another life lesson that if you need money ask for it. His first taste of entrepreneurship came when he sold sweets to afford his school lunch because he was 20p short. But then his supply stopped. When he asked his mother for the extra amount, she gave it to him without hesitation.

"When I started in property, I remembered that and just started asking investors for funds. If you don't ask, you don't get."

After leaving school, the former St John the Baptist pupil went into the building trade briefly as an apprentice. It gave him a basic understanding about constructing a house from the ground up. He left because he did not want to be an employee, but it was an invaluable experience.

Then with the financial crisis in 2008, Josh saw his opportunity to get onto the property ladder as house prices in Britain plummeted. He wrote a business plan and shared it with potential investors.

"I had strict criteria and got my first property way below market value."

Today Josh is a familiar figure on the networking circuit with his trademark trilby hat and is a prolific negotiator. In one day alone, on his way to a meeting with his mentor, Samuel Leeds, Josh made two telephone calls and raised £155,000. He then had an offer of £145,000 accepted on a two-bedroom flat worth £175,000 in Bristol where he has already pulled off many deals.

After installing new furniture and a boiler, the plan is to rent out the apartment. He says this will produce a rapid return on investment of at least 30 per cent.

But being a property entrepreneur has not been all plain sailing. Three years ago, Josh bought a house in Wolverhampton. He planned to spend some money improving it, rent it to multiple tenants and then refinance it. But a few months into the project his mum died. With his dad ill at home as well, it was enough to take his 'eye off the ball' and the builder abandoned the project.

Josh had bought the house deal from Samuel and turned to him for help to get the scheme back on track. With the multi-millionaire's assistance, the house is now another of Josh's success stories. The property is being rented out for £2,000 a month.

He says he is also hugely grateful to Samuel for 're-energising' him and increasing his knowledge of the property sector when he attended the company's free crash course in 2016.

"People might think having dyslexia would hamper me, but I believe it's made me a natural problem solver. Sometimes I can't believe I've raised over £1m in private finance. It's been built on work, trust and relationships. To be able to ring someone up and say 'hey, could you lend me £150,000' and they say 'no worries it'll be in your account tomorrow' is amazing.

"I've never done a deal that has lost me money and I've paid back every penny that I have borrowed from investors when the money was due."

Samuel Leeds said: "What Josh has achieved has been incredible, especially when you think he has never spent any of his own money. He has had to get through some seriously hard times, but it's just made him stronger.

"He is living proof that you don't need £100,000 to make money from property. You just raise the money."

Josh, a director of 2B Property Ltd, now intends to treat himself to his dream car - a Ferrari F355 Spider sports car.

"I haven't bought one before because I keep buying houses, but I'm a bit of a petrolhead."

JOSH'S TIPS

"Once you are established, employ someone to help you with administrative tasks. I have someone in the Philippines who does all my admin, including handling my emails and invoices. I found this person through a friend. I also sometimes source property deals for investors. I have a group of sourcers, plus my virtual assistant sends me deals every week that meet my criteria. The way I operate has become faster and better as a result and allowed me to focus on networking and attracting investors."

"The crash course was awesome. I would totally recommend it. Come along if you're going to do it. If not, don't come to it. Being a successful property entrepreneur involves work and it is not easy but you can do it. I started with no property experience and no money and I'm building up a portfolio."

"With training, be careful where put your money and make sure the trainer is doing what they preach. Samuel lives and breathes property. He is buying deals all the time. He makes everything simplified to the point where you believe you can do it. I wouldn't be where I am now without him. He has been a key influence in my life. He gave me motivation to do things I wasn't doing. His energy is immense. You go away on a high from the crash course."

"I go to national network meetings for property entrepreneurs where I pick up contacts and share ideas. I collected 147 business cards out of 300 people in the room at one networking event. It's so important for people to be aware of you and your service."

Chapter 5 – Alasdair Cunningham

'Sceptical Scot' who became a walking, talking testament to Samuel Leeds' teachings

At the start of his property journey, former mechanic Alasdair Cunningham doubted whether Samuel Leeds' property investing techniques actually worked. As Samuel once described him, he was a 'sceptical Scot.'

The father-of-two was also at a low ebb in his life at the time. He managed, however, to overcome his misgivings to become not only a prolific deal sourcer but also Samuel Leeds' business partner and trusted lead trainer.

After joining the Property Investors Academy, Alasdair set up a deal sourcing company with Samuel as a co-director. Within two years the Scotsman was earning more than £30,000 a month on top of a monthly rental income of around £3,000.

His star has continued to rise since. In 2019, Alasdair sold more than 220 property deals to investors. He has also become a regular fixture at Samuel's events, inspiring thousands of people with his story of how he became an entrepreneur.

Along the way he and his mentor even came face to face with death after being flung from a boat during a team-building exercise in Africa. Thankfully, they both lived to tell the tale and have gone on to become friends, so much so that Samuel sees him as a brother.

Alasdair says he still pinches himself when he looks back on how his fortunes have changed so dramatically and how different he is as a person now.

"Samuel and I met in mid 2016. I was inspired by him but also very sceptical. But then I got involved and I played full out. I got one property and then another one, then did some lease options and deal sourcing. Now I've got a property portfolio and a passive income. The deal sourcing business is systemised and I'm training and speaking on the very stages I was sceptical about."

Alasdair might have had his reservations early on about Samuel, but he got a taste of how property can create wealth when he sold his ex-council home in Bedfordshire under the tenant Right to Buy scheme. He made £100,000 from the sale and moved with his family to Corby in Northamptonshire where he was able to buy a much bigger house.

Having previously run a commercial vehicle maintenance business, Alasdair bought a franchise from a tools company but disliked the work and gave it up. For a while he suffered from severe depression brought on by the anxiety of feeling he was a failure, despite being happily married and having a comfortable standard of living.

Alasdair first saw Samuel on TV, on *The Week the Landlords Moved In*, the BBC One series which challenged successful landlords to live for seven days in one of their rentals, on their tenant's budget.

'Mesmerised' by how someone who was still only in his twenties could be doing so well, Alasdair went along to the free Property Investors Crash Course to find out more. On the first day he thought Samuel was making it sound all too easy. Alasdair sat there with his arms folded, while everyone around him clapped. The following day the would-be investors were offered the chance to enrol on the *Never Use Your Own Money Again* course for £2,000. Alasdair was put off by the cost, but his wife Lisa persuaded him to sign up for it.

After that he booked himself onto the *Deal Finding Extravaganza*, although he again had cold feet.

"I was still a little bit sceptical. I arrived and registered but then my nerves and anxiety kicked in. There were 25 people there and I thought, 'Is it really that easy?'"

He says his whole negative mindset came back when he arrived at the venue. "I thought this is going to be a waste of three days and I got back in my car and left. I phoned my wife and said we've spent £2,000 but it's not going to work. She said don't be stupid get back there."

In the evening, he was relaxing with the other delegates, chatting over a drink, when at one point he found himself sitting on his own. Seeing this, Samuel came over to talk to him.

"That was the moment where I thought, he's not a bad guy. He's not just trying to sell to me. He does actually care."

The next day Alasdair spoke to the Property Investors founder about the academy and the different training modules.

"I remember I was shaking his hand and wouldn't let go."

Samuel recalls their meeting too: "He said just look me in the eye and tell me this is true! I said I can't promise it's going to work for you, but it works."

Originally from Callander, near Glasgow, Alasdair blames his doubts on his upbringing. "I've been brought up that if it sounds too good to be true it always is. You're led to believe if you want anything in life you have to work your ass off for it – physical hard labour. I come from a family of labourers – joiners, builders, carpenters. I was a bus and coach mechanic. I was getting filthy every single day and working hard to make money.

"Then Samuel showed me a way of working hard but combining it with working smarter."

Alasdair became the 'golden boy' of the academy. He sold nine deals in as many weeks, making £27,000. However, his pessimism returned during a day spent viewing properties in Hull. He saw ten houses but dismissed them all because he thought they needed too much work doing on them.

"I know now they were all perfect buy, refurbish, refinance opportunities but at the time I hadn't done the training to realise that."

He sat in his car with viewing forms and notes scattered over the back seat and said to himself: 'I told you this doesn't work.' However, on the last viewing he was informed there was another property he could see the next day.

"I wasn't going to stay overnight but thought whatever it takes and went to the viewing. It was a fully refurbed four-bed HMO and I sold that to an investor two days later. That made me think, actually this does work if you put the effort in. I'd nearly given up."

Whatever It Takes is the title of his new book which sets out in easy-to-follow steps how to become a deal sourcer. He called it that because Samuel told Alasdair his success was down to doing 'whatever it takes.'

Whilst the two men are firm friends these days, they nearly got off on the wrong foot. Alasdair had been advised that if he brought any deals to the table, Property Investors would sell them for him. However, there was a misunderstanding over the level of the commission. By this time, he had sourced seven deals and was expecting a hefty fee.

To resolve the situation, Samuel rang Alasdair on a Sunday and said that if he came to his office with one property deal the following morning, he would help him to sell it to an investor. Alasdair exceeded his target by bringing him not just one deal but three which he had already been working on.

"I brought three deals because I like to over-deliver on everything I do, and I was being cheeky because I knew he might sell all three.

"We looked at the deals, did due diligence, and sent an email out to his investors' list. Then we just literally held up his phone as it went ping, ping, ping constantly from investors texting and saying show me the deal.

"By eleven o'clock we'd sold them to investors, the money was in the bank and we were sat in the pub having lunch. Seeing that was the biggest motivation I ever needed because I was thinking, I work my ass off to earn £2,500 a month and I've done a deal making £2,500 in an hour."

Samuel showed Alasdair the whole system of how to find investors and devised a programme for him which has now been adapted into the company's *Deal Selling Masterclass*.

Following his unofficial masterclass, Alasdair went 'crazy on networking,' speaking at events all over the country to find investors. He drove to Cornwall for one meeting after being told there would be 40 people there – only to find six when he arrived. It did not matter to him because he was again prepared to do 'whatever it takes.' With Samuel coaching him how to speak in front of an audience, Alasdair built an investors' list and found deals.

One Sunday morning, he set out to see two houses in Lincoln and ended up being away from home for a week because an agent offered to show him more properties. He viewed 52 houses and sold four of them to investors while he was on the road – two of them when he was on top of the Pennines.

During the same week he also negotiated a lease option agreement on a property and now has a small portfolio of them. Two of Samuel's staff members became tenants in one of his first lease options in Wolverhampton. He plans to exercise his option to buy another one in Hull in 2021, ahead of the agreement's expiry date.

As part of the arrangement, he pays the owner of the four-bed HMO £420 a month and then rents out the rooms at a higher rate and keeps the profit. Up until the Covid-19 crisis it was making £1,250 to £1,300 a month, he says. The Polish tenants returned home when the coronavirus pandemic hit. As a result, the house stood empty for around four months but is tenanted once more.

Alasdair became financially free in just three months and has gone on to systemise his deal sourcing company, Better Sourced Limited, by appointing a manager and a small team of employees and co-sourcers to run it. He calls them every day and also holds a weekly management meeting. This lasts about ten minutes when he examines the key performance indicators, which show whether objectives are being met, and then takes 'a nice cheque.' He has done business with investors from Britain, as well as Hong Kong, Bahrain and Switzerland, all seeking to invest in the UK housing market.

It is a passive income stream not only for him but also for Samuel who jokes that he 'hit the jackpot with Alasdair Cunningham', especially with more juicy deals on the horizon. The 38-year-old has also purchased a four-bed, end terrace house in Bedford for £210,000. He completed the sale before an Article 4 restriction came into force which limits the number of HMOs allowed in the area. He was aware the rule was about to come in and got permission beforehand to convert the property into a five-bed house share.

The refurbishment cost £50,000 including rectifying some structural issues. Once the work is finished, he expects it to be revalued at £360,000. This will enable him to pull out all his money by refinancing the mortgage and then letting the accommodation.

"I've already got someone to take it off my hands and give me £2,500 a month, or I can rent it privately and get £3,500 a month."

As Samuel puts it, that is financial freedom from just one deal!

A total of 43 people viewed the house before Alasdair but were put off because the upper floor was held up by Acrow Props. The quote to fix it was £36,000. With his connections at the academy and knowledge, Alasdair got the job done for less than £4,000.

"People say the academy is expensive, but I saved three times the cost of that in one deal."

An important part of Samuel's life is his charity work, particularly in rural Africa. In 2018, he invited Alasdair and a select group of Property Investors Academy members to accompany him on a mission bringing fresh water to remote Ugandan villages. During the trip Alasdair was able to observe first-hand the impact of some of his teacher's projects, including the building of wells and improving educational facilities.

It was during this trip, however, that both men almost died while white water rafting on the River Nile. The experience had been organised to help the team get to know each another and prepare them for the challenges ahead. It went disastrously wrong when their boat capsized in dangerous rapids.

Samuel shattered his kneecap on rocks and had to undergo emergency surgery in Uganda after losing a quarter of his blood. Alasdair was badly bruised after plunging down two waterfalls and being swept along the river for nearly a mile before being rescued. The rest of the group escaped with minor injuries.

"I really thought I was going to drown. I still have flashbacks now and have to see a chiropractor three times a week for a twisted pelvis, but Samuel was in a much worse state. Even so, his main concern was for his team."

After waiting three hours to be picked up, they were crammed into the back of a six-seater minibus. Alasdair was underneath Samuel supporting his leg.

"Every time we went over a bump he was screaming in agony. He started passing out and I was shouting at him to wake up, you're not going here. It was the scariest moment of my life."

Despite this setback, they all carried on with the mission after Samuel gave them a rousing motivational talk from his hospital bed about the importance of not giving up, even in adversity. Samuel's brother Russell took over as leader.

Alasdair is so passionate about his business he even completed deals on his mobile phone, again while on a minibus, just days after the accident. On a 10-hour journey from Jinja to a village, near Kabale, he sent out his usual weekly sales email to investors informing them of the latest property deals he had available.

"I ran up a phone bill of just under £400 but luckily I made £5,000 in sales, so it didn't matter. We sold two deals. I couldn't believe it.
"Both deals were for houses in the same street in Hull. I sent out the invoices and terms and conditions, checked my bank account and saw the investors had paid the money. It just proves you can do this type of property dealing from anywhere in the world."

During his stay in Uganda Alasdair was also one of the judges of a 'Dragons' Den' type event aimed at offering free business loans to local people with the best commercial ideas.

On the way back to England he and his party travelled to Johannesburg in South Africa to have dinner with Robert Kiyosaki, author of the international, best-selling business book *Rich Dad, Poor Dad,* as a pre-arranged present from Samuel.

Alasdair has now completed hundreds of deals and says he still 'works his ass off but for a damn sight more money.'

He adds: "I would pay for the additional training ten times over because of how much I've made, the connections and friends, the knowledge and mindset shift. It's changed everything for me. The biggest change is I believe in myself. When you believe in yourself, you're unstoppable."

With Samuel's help, he has also become a confident speaker and trainer.
"I've always thought I was destined to be on stage. Ten to fifteen years ago I saw someone delivering a seminar and thought that's what I wanted to do, help people. Then I saw Samuel on stage helping people and thought

that's amazing. I give everything to my training. You see normal everyday people transforming their lives by taking action and learning the skills that rich people don't want to teach. That's why I do what I do."

Alasdair also appears in a regular podcast with Property Investors CEO Russell Leeds.

Samuel is glowing in his praise of his former student: "I'm incredibly proud of what Alasdair's done and who he's become. He's a walking, talking testimonial and I believe he's only just getting started. He's the only person I trust to run the Samuel Leeds training events. He gets tremendous customer feedback, and his book is fabulous.

"Sometimes people criticise me for making it look too easy which I take as a compliment. It's like saying Cristiano Ronaldo makes football look too easy. Whatever you do in life is going to take hard work."

ALASDAIR'S TIPS

"Property is about people and relationships, so when you meet agents speak to them and listen because they've got problems and you can fix them."

"I keep money in the bank for when I have void periods and would advise anyone else to do the same."

"I've had people message me saying how long does the crash course last and where is it? It doesn't matter. You have to do whatever it takes."

"Enrol on the free crash course. It's awesome value and you get to see deals being done live on stage, as well as having a go yourself."

"Get in the game. Go out looking for deals – not just on sites like Rightmove. Get physically out there and actually see the property you are intending to source."

"Go networking so that you get to know agents and people in your industry. This will bring you good deals and put you in touch with tradesmen if a property needs to be renovated."
"Listen to the vendor's story. A lot of lease option agreements come that way. If they are struggling to sell, they might consider allowing you to

rent their house in return for a guaranteed monthly payment and an option to buy in future. You can make a profit that way and have a potentially good investment on your hands."

"Don't listen to your negative voice saying I'm not deserving of this. Just go out there and do it."

Chapter 6 – Mark Parham

Businessman earns money even while he is sleeping from one HMO with ROI of more than 27 per cent

Businessman Mark Parham had no hesitation in investing in property after coming across Samuel Leeds on YouTube. First, he watched his videos and then he read his book, *Buy Low Rent High*.

Having done his research and been convinced by what he read, Mark jumped straight in and bought a house share through Samuel's sourcing company in 2017.

He took out a mortgage to buy the three-bedroomed house in Sheffield for £100,000. Then he spent £9,800 on converting it into a four-bed and renovating the interior, including the bathroom. Within five weeks the property was fully let.

Shortly after the first tenant moved in, a leak was discovered in the roof. It cost him £1,400 to re-felt it but the work came with a 10-year warranty. He also had to fit fire doors, a new fire alarm and a fuse board which added £450 to the bill.

After paying legal fees and stamp duty, plus a mortgage of £128 with a 1.69 per cent interest rate, the father-of-two from Didcot in Oxfordshire says he is left with a monthly profit of £920.

"I bought it completely blind, but I've done business with a lot of people and everything the company was saying made sense. I paid a £3,500 sourcing fee which was good value for all the work they'd done in finding and packaging the deal and talking me through the process.

"I was a little bit nervous because you never really know if it's going to be profitable, but when the figures all make sense it's time to take action. If you wait, the opportunity passes you by. With the formula Samuel teaches, you can stress test properties like this quite high before they become loss-making.

"The return on investment works out at 27.4 per cent which includes the unexpected roof repair and the small cost of having a monthly cleaner to maintain the place to a high standard and keep an eye it. I was told by the sourcing company that the ROI would between 25 to 30 per cent, so I'm happy with that."

Mark achieved a slightly higher rent than had been predicted by ensuring his accommodation was decorated to a high standard. He brought in painters to give it a fresh look and create a feature wall. New furniture was also installed, along with art and a TV on the wall in the lounge.

"There were 300 adverts for spare rooms in Sheffield when I was doing my project. I needed mine to look like it was the best. I could have spent £3,000 on a new kitchen and £6,000 on a new bathroom but that would have been out of proportion with a £100,000 house. It was enough to bring in good furniture, decorate it nicely and put up a £50 piece of art on the wall."

He tested the market by putting up an advert for the rooms to see how much he might be able to rent them out for. Within five hours five enquiries came in. This led him to set the rent for the four rooms at £1,475 a month.

On top of this passive income, the house has already gone up in value – a similar property in worse condition on the same road sold for 10 per cent more than the figure Mark paid.

Mark hopes to refinance the house within a year and pull out most, if not all, of his money to reinvest again in more HMOs in Sheffield.

He added: "I absolutely love investing. Savings is for mugs. Investing is where the money is. It's just so liberating to see the money roll in when you're doing nothing towards it.

"I recently worked out what I earn per hour even when I'm sleeping. It's really reassuring to know that while you're asleep you're still earning really well."

Samuel said: "Mark did everything literally by my book. He's a natural businessman. He didn't know the area particularly well and had never owned any properties in the north but trusted the formula. He also used our mortgage broker which means he's paying a very low mortgage. That's helped him to make this investment so successful. He's a big thinker and doesn't do anything by halves."

MARK'S TIPS

"My background is in recruitment, marketing and sales. I've run my own taxi business and online marketing business and more recently a fairly large ground transportation business. I'm also involved in a few other projects. I've got a varied, rounded business background, mostly around looking for opportunities to create value.

I think the reason the HMO market is so strong and such a good business model is that you take a product and you add value to it. That's the whole definition of how you create wealth by adding value. I regard my tenants as clients and I'm the business owner. I provide them with the service they expect. The house is the product. So make sure you get good contractors in. If you build a bad product, you're not going to have many happy customers."

"If you go into a house renovation project thinking how cheaply you can do it for and you don't budget for contingencies, that's a really dangerous starting point because you need to be able to finish the project and rent out the house. I would recommend having a contingency fund of about £2,000. It's a problem if you need a roof repair, for example, and haven't got a contingency."

"One thing I've learnt as an investor is that my income has probably trebled over the last year, but my expenses have stayed the same. I live a very comfortable life, but I've been enjoying investing. I think when your passion is creating wealth then actually you can do it very quickly."

"Get a good accountant and mortgage broker and pay them per transaction rather than employing them. The old adage with insurance is that it seems expensive until you need it. It's like that with accountancy. It's really expensive until the accountant, or broker, saves you all that money. They might not save you anything in the first instance but then it comes in big lumps."

"If I was starting out from scratch, I might not pick Sheffield. It's a little bit more expensive than other areas and there's an article 4 direction in place just down the road, which restricts the number of HMOs allowed, but I've got my power team there and people I trust. You have to find your own area for investing."

Chapter 7 – Anthony Wilmott

First winner of The Eviction turns £20,000 prize into property gold!

If anyone can prove that Property Investors' training is transformational it is Anthony Wilmott. Just a few years ago he had sunk to the depths of despair due to problems in his personal and professional life. His fortunes changed dramatically when he attended the crash course and later signed up for the academy.

The former supermarket manager and qualified teacher went on to win £20,000 in *The Eviction*, an Apprentice-style competition established by the company's founder, Samuel Leeds, to reward his best students.

Anthony used his prize money wisely to gain an ongoing benefit. He put some of the cash into renovating his old house, as well as furnishing five lease option apartments, to generate a rental income for himself.

He followed that up by joining forces with another contestant to make over £200,000 from deal sourcing in six months. Now they are collaborating on seven-figure development deals and have raised more than £1m in investor finance.

The fire that fuelled his desire to turn around his life by becoming a property entrepreneur continues to burn within him, driving him on to new successes. It was this same enthusiasm which resulted in him being invited to compete in *The Eviction* in 2019. He was always on the front row at academy training events and the first to put up his hand when asked a question.

His commitment and passion impressed his trainers. Along with eleven other candidates from around the country, Anthony arrived at a moated mansion in Staffordshire to compete in a series of challenges based around different property investment strategies.

Two days before the tests began, Anthony moved into a new house. After handing over the keys to his partner, he said: "I'll see you in a month because I am winning when I come back."

His confidence paid off. After each challenge, one contestant was evicted from their room within the medieval walls of Caverswall Castle. Finally, Anthony triumphed after presenting a business plan about how he would spend his winnings.

It was a victory for him in so many ways after years of struggling with his mental health. In 2018, he hit his lowest point after a previous partner left him and he faced losing his job.

"I literally had nothing," he recalls. "I was stuck in this house I couldn't really afford to run on my own and then I got told I was potentially going to be made redundant as well. It was tough. Then things started breaking in the house and I didn't have the money to fix them.

"That was a rock bottom moment for me, the moment that made me pick up the phone to my brother. I need to know what's next because if I don't know what's next, there isn't going to be a next. That was a scary thought."

His brother, who was a self-employed electrician at the time, said Anthony could come and work for him, but in the long term he was looking to get into property.

"I thought that sounds amazing, but I can barely keep the roof over my head, let alone buy another house."

At his brother's suggestion, he watched Samuel's YouTube videos. At first, Anthony was unimpressed.

"I thought who is this absolutely crazy guy I'm watching these videos of? This isn't really for me."

However, the more he delved into the subject the more it piqued his interest and so he decided to book himself and his brother onto the free, two-day *Property Investors Crash Course* in May 2018.

"The crash course completely opened my eyes. I was going to these free events, like the crash course and other networking events, and thinking this is really achievable. Coming from a position of having no money it is doable, if you can network and make the right connections."

Anthony had been expecting Samuel to appear on a video and someone else to be hosting the actual event. He was stunned when Samuel walked out on stage.

"I was like, oh my God, he's actually here. He's taken the time to come out and teach us this. I said to my brother I'm going to be friends with that guy."

After the crash course Anthony did 'everything in his power,' to take advantage of Samuel's advanced training. Even a car crash on his way to the *Deal Finding Extravaganza* course failed to prevent him from arriving on time. He ditched his vehicle in a service station and called his mother to drive him there.

"Nothing was going to stop me from pushing forward with this. I'd made commitments to myself that I was going to get into property. I could see the position I'd come from in rented accommodation and how I now wanted to provide great houses for people. I was really making it my mission. Ever since then I've gone at it 100-mile-an-hour and never looked back."

He used his credit card to pay for the deal finding course and was soon gaining invaluable tips from Samuel about which strategies to pursue. Anthony had been planning to build a portfolio of buy-to-lets and take on buy, refurbish, refinance projects. Samuel advised him instead to focus initially on strategies, such as rent-to-rent and deal sourcing, to bring in money, and then chase his long-term goals.

"Coming to that event was life-changing, even in the first ten minutes. Delegates were asked what their strategy was. Being always the first to put my hand up, I told Samuel what mine was. He said that was stupid. I was never going to get where I wanted to be because I was looking at a long-term strategy when I didn't have the finance. That lightbulb moment gave me the motivation to do it in the way he suggested."

A month after attending the *Deal Finding Extravaganza* in September 2018, Anthony co-sourced his first deal. Samuel had told him that if he viewed 40 properties in a fortnight, he would give him £1,000 to fix his car. Anthony narrowly missed his target but only because he wanted to concentrate his efforts on selling the deal. He earned the £1,000 by passing on the deal to a sourcer who sold it to an investor.

In January 2019, he took out a loan to join the Property Investors Academy after selling two more deals. "I love the free crash course and free networking events. They're a great eye-opener but I wanted to be around people who had invested in their education."

At the time Anthony had no savings but calculated that he had a salary coming in every month and could afford to take out a loan to cover the fee.

"It was a tough commitment to make but the pain of doing that is what drove me to push forwards."

Samuel says would-be property investors have to decide themselves whether or not to sign up for his paid-for training.

"People sometimes say to me, you should be choosier about who you accept onto your training. I've spent so many hundreds of hours weighing up that comment but it's impossible to know who's going to be successful and who's not.

"Sometimes we have doctors who come to the crash course and have loads of money. Then a year later I check in with them and they've done nothing. Other times we have people come on who have got nothing but do great things, like me when I started. I was a working class teenager with nothing. I could very easily have been turned away at the door."

He adds: "No one told Anthony to get a loan or put something on his credit card. All we did was tell him how much it cost. Then he made that decision. He put the effort in and made it work."

It was through the Property Investors Academy that Anthony met James Armstrong. They bounced well off each other and started looking at deals together, including a commercial to residential venture. Although it did not come to fruition, it familiarised them with the process of dealing with planners and architects.

Then in April 2019 they were both chosen as contestants in *The Eviction*. During one challenge Anthony's team negotiated lease option agreements on five apartments in Derby. After the competition finished, Anthony, James and two other contestants, Hannah Mills and John Raybould, formed a joint venture to rent them out as furnished accommodation.

It was the start of a frenzied period of activity. Anthony had previously taken on two serviced apartments in Sheffield and with his brother secured another two in the city to add to an ever-expanding portfolio. Anthony had separately completed two buy, refurbish, refinance projects and James also began searching for deals they could sell to investors.

"After leaving The Eviction we made over £200,00 in deal sourcing in a six-month period. We were grafting hard. We managed refurbishments for our investors along the way."

Recently, the joint venture partners decided to hand back the five lease option apartments in the wake of the coronavirus outbreak and changing market conditions.

"We needed to change the terms of the contract to make it financially beneficial to us and the owner because the cash flow wasn't quite where we wanted it to be. Unfortunately, they didn't want to negotiate the contract, so we made the business decision to step away from it."

Anthony also dropped two of the four rent-to-serviced accommodation apartments in Sheffield for the same reason. The other two are in the city centre and have been rented out during the pandemic for short and long stays. However, the Covid crisis has forced them to reconsider their strategy.

"There are going to be a lot of changes with planning regulations and permitted development, so we've decided to change our strategy to more commercial conversions and development."

In spite of the coronavirus outbreak and lockdowns, 2020 was a busy year of finding land deals and development projects to pursue. Anthony is joint venturing with James and another investor on a scheme to convert a redundant pub into six apartments. Their most ambitious project, however, is a massive redevelopment of a Grade II listed building. Anthony described it as his 'secret project.' It was recently unveiled as a derelict castle, enjoying a fabulous location near the Welsh coast, which will be converted into apartments. They have linked up with David Taylor, a structural engineer who was also a member of the Property Investors Academy, to help them bring the fire-damaged castle back to life.

"Even Samuel didn't know what it was. We took him there and his jaw hit the floor when he saw it. We also presented him with a gift for all the help and inspiration he has given us."

On the development front, the three of them are planning to build 14 houses on land in the North West. They raised the funds straight away, he says, having had their confidence boosted by seeing a renowned builder developing a large plot across the road.

Life has had its peaks and troughs for 35-year-old Anthony, but it is property which has kept him going. At his lowest point, he sat in his bath, filling up a bucket with hot water to wash himself because he had no heating in his house.

"I remember it to this day – and this is the fuel that keeps me going – thinking is this really it? Have I worked my whole life for this? In 2020, I lost my dad. He was a great person. He was a complete rock and supported me the whole way through my life and then all that's left is paperwork and closing accounts. All his life amounts to is the memories we've got with him. I don't want to leave that for my daughter, my mum, my partner. I want to leave a legacy, and that is what drives me through all the tough stuff every single day."

He adds: "My daughter was born in September 2020. She is the best thing that ever happened to me and I'm excited about the future."

Samuel says: "Anthony came to me with nothing and has grown to the point now where he is doing massive deals. He's made money from deal sourcing, became financially free from his rent-to-rents and he's got lease options. Anthony is the perfect example of the progression on the property journey. I even go to him for property advice now!

"He also spends so much time sitting with people on the academy, mentoring and sharing his experiences and taking people on sites. I'm so thankful for what he's given back to the business."

ANTHONY'S TIPS

"My best advice is to make sure you network. I've become part of an accountability group with some of the people on the academy. They helped me through to where I am now. We keep each other accountable and we help each other push forward."

"If you want to get into property and are serious about doing it, the Property Investors Crash Course is a great place to start. If it's a whim, then it's not for you. The academy builds on the knowledge you get at the crash course and gives you real in-depth detail about all the specific strategies."

"When you joint venture with people, you might think you know them, but even when you do, make sure you define each other's roles and responsibilities."

"You must be prepared to work hard to succeed. If you're not willing to do that, then property investing is not for you."

"What I've learned about myself during my property journey is that I can doubt myself an awful lot. When I take that away and stop doubting myself and just take action, then I do a lot more."

"Most people should start off by building a good foundation of income-generating properties and not over-stretch themselves in deals that are way above their heads. Having said that, if you see something you think would be a good investment you can pursue it with a good joint venture partner, so long as you have a solid income, proceed very carefully and have had the right training. Just remember that these are long-term strategies and not something you should be expecting to make millions from overnight. Generally speaking the best advice is to start small and build from there."

Chapter 8 – Hannah Mills

Hannah lost The Eviction, then won big time in property

Hannah Mills never lost a single challenge in *The Eviction 2019* – Property Investors' Apprentice-style competition. In the end, however, her business plan was judged to be riskier than that of the eventual winner and she missed out on the £20,000 prize.

You cannot keep a good woman down, though, and Hannah vowed to get the money back through property investing. Since then, she has managed to deliver on that promise many times over.

The 28-year-old now co-owns a sourcing business bringing in around £25,000 a month, has her own rent-to-rent portfolio and is involved in a string of other big money ventures.

Hannah's love of property goes back a long way. When she was growing up, she used to sit down with her mum and dad and watch TV shows about doing up houses and selling them at a profit. It gave her a desire to become a property entrepreneur herself, but then she took the 'safe route' and became a qualified solicitor instead.

The attraction of having a well-paid job soon paled, though, when she found herself commuting five hours a day. On the train home Hannah started scrolling through Facebook and found Samuel Leeds' YouTube channel. She then enrolled on one of his crash courses in London and joined the Property Investors Academy in February 2019.

A few months later she was offered a life-changing opportunity to take part in *The Eviction* while working as a solicitor in Bristol. The problem was that she could get any annual leave. She solved her dilemma by handing in her notice.

Her colleagues laughed at her decision to quit. And it was a courageous step. At the time she was earning £47,000 a year but was convinced she could succeed as a property entrepreneur.

By then Hannah was already used to risk-taking, having borrowed £24,000 on credit cards to start a rent-to-serviced accommodation business.

"I didn't just quit my job with nothing coming in. I had three properties in Cambridge that I was managing. From the income they were producing per month I could afford my liabilities, so it wasn't a case of I'm just going to do it. I'd already had a bit of training and a plan," Hannah explains.

Having landed her first 'big ticket job' at the age of 25 and bought a house, she had no savings. Her credit rating, however, was good because of her job and this allowed her to secure low percentage loans.

Hannah picked up valuable tips about property investing from watching Samuel Leeds' YouTube videos and came to the crash course wanting to find out more. There was a surprise in store when in the first five minutes Samuel asked each member of the audience to massage the person on their left.

"To be honest, I was wondering what this was about, but it's very much about losing your inhibitions. We're all on the same page, with everyone enjoying themselves, and you just buy into it. I felt energised.

"You can't come away from that place and not feel energised and to think, do you know what, I'm going to go out and kick a***. I really enjoyed it."

An added benefit was that she met her future business partner, Gwyn Thomas, at the crash course. Both had travelled a long way to be at the event – Gwyn from Russia, where he was working at the time, and Hannah from her home in South Wales.

A few months later she left her job and took another gamble by investing £12,000 in the Property Investors Academy.

"My partner Cori said to me the other day where do you see yourself in property and I said I'm going to be a millionaire. She said how do you know? I said, I just know."

It was that same belief in herself which drove her to leave the legal profession. "I knew it was the right decision. I had to know about property and be around people, living and breathing it because I was so passionate about it. I knew I wouldn't fail.

"Some people may see it as a risk. For me it was just a stepping-stone."

Students on the academy are given a solid grounding in making money from the housing market, learning all the different strategies available to investors, including rent-to-rents.

It was this strategy which Hannah concentrated on. Describing how it works, she says:

"Basically, you take a landlord's property and you rent it from them. Then you re-rent it out again. Some people call it sub-letting. If you're dealing with rent-to-HMOs, it is sub-letting. With rent-to-serviced accommodation it's different because you're not actually putting tenants in, you're putting in guests. The idea of it is very simple. You rent it or book it out under your business."

Hannah could not afford to pay sourcers to find deals for her when she started out, so she did it herself, negotiating corporate management agreements on three apartments. It saved her a lot of money, but she admits to making 'so many big mistakes.' She spent about £8,000 on each property before she could begin making any money out of them.

Nevertheless, it turned out to be a good move. Two years later Hannah handed back one of the properties – a one-bedroom flat – and replaced it with a four-bedroom house. The rent and liabilities of the two properties are similar, but she earns more from the house.

Her initial rent-to-rents are still making a profit of £2,000-£3,000 per month – even during the Covid crisis, she says.

"One of them is a two-bedroom cottage and for one month I got a £3,000 booking which is crazy in the middle of a pandemic when some areas are really struggling."

The location and knowing the market have been vital in helping her to survive through such challenging times. AstraZeneca, makers of the coronavirus vaccine, moved its global headquarters to Cambridge in 2016, bringing in large numbers of employees looking for accommodation. Other hi-tech firms have also relocated to the area in recent years. This has driven up demand in the rental sector, already bolstered by the presence of world-famous institutions, such as Cambridge University and Addenbrookes Hospital.

Samuel says a lot of people are sceptical about rent-to-rents, but a lot of his students pursue the strategy successfully. For Hannah the model was ideal because she wanted quick cash flow to repay her loans. She also worked out that it would generate more revenue than simply buying one property.

"I thought if I can take a property and I can earn, let's say £1,500 a month from it, or I can buy one property and earn £230 after management fees, then that was an absolute no brainer.

"If I can make £1,500 per month for three to five years, I've got a deposit there for a house. I wanted to scale my business and I thought the best way to do that would be to do rent-to-rents – get loads of cash flow, invest the profits and keep doing it, instead of having one property, waiting for a couple of years, getting capital appreciation, remortgaging it and doing it that way."

She learnt a lot from taking part in *The Eviction* which took place in a moated castle in Staffordshire.

"We had challenges pretty much every day and whoever failed on those challenges got evicted from the castle. I genuinely would say it was life-changing because I learnt so much from the different tasks."

During her stay at Caverswall Castle, Hannah was involved in deal selling and refurbishing an HMO and would constantly be picking the brains of other contestants. She also gained advice from Samuel and spent a lot of time with Alasdair Cunningham, Property Investors' lead trainer, who was mentoring her team.

Hannah admits that it still hurts her today that she failed to win the competition.

"I was quite upset because I really wanted to succeed, but I was determined to make that £20,000 back which I did, and some more!"

There were other compensations. The eventual winner, Anthony Wilmott, and another contestant, James Armstrong, have become two of her closest friends in property. They have also co-written a book with Samuel, entitled *A Guide to Making Property Compliance Easy*!

After *The Eviction* Hannah and her partner Gwyn, who is based in Essex, began growing their sourcing business and also buying properties. By the end of 2019 they were earning around £8,000 a month from selling deals to investors. Since then, they have massively scaled up the operation by employing staff to source more deals and increase turnover.

"We're doing on average seven to 10 deals a month at the moment, with each one worth around £3,250," says Hannah.

Their business, Bespoke Sourcing, has also managed to attract foreign investors who buy four or five deals at a time.

There are five employees on the payroll. They include women who worked for top five Magic Circle law firms in London but then left their jobs to have children. They now work remotely for Bespoke Sourcing.

"They've got that knowledge and understanding of big companies and that's really driven the business forward," Hannah adds.

Another recruit is her partner Cori, formerly captain of Cardiff City's women's football team who played for Wales and has joined the business on a full-time basis – along with someone who 'dips in and out' finding development opportunities.

Hannah is also engaged in several joint venture projects, co-owning four houses in one street alone, including one which is being converted from two to four bedrooms.

She bought the house with James Armstrong for £69,000. The refurbishment is costing around £30,000. Once the work is finished, Hannah expects to sell it for £145,000 to £150,000. This will leave them with at least £45,000 to put into other projects.

Hannah then bought the house next door which she managed to secure below market value. The plan is to refinance that one, pull out all the money and then rent it out for about £675 per calendar month, giving a monthly profit of around £475.

After establishing her rent-to-rent portfolio and finding lots of excellent investment opportunities, it became a natural progression to move into deal sourcing. There was one deal, however, which was so good that she wanted to keep it. She found a house for sale in Mountain Ash in the

South Wales valleys and suggested to her business partner that they start a buy, refurbish, refinance portfolio.

He agreed straight away. Hannah obtained investment cash to buy the property and they added a third bedroom to increase the value.

One of the investors was a fellow academy member whom she met on the *Deal Finding Extravaganza* training programme. That particular investor keeps giving them money and in return he receives a fixed return.

Hannah and Gwyn have six refurbishment projects about to get underway for their own portfolio and numerous investor properties which are being renovated. Hannah, who is supervising the work, says she is so busy she is running out of builders.

They also have a rent-to-rent in Newport, plus a seven-bed house share which they turned into a mini apartment hotel with two kitchens and bathrooms and seven en suite double rooms. Unfortunately, the Covid-19 pandemic put a halt to their plans.

"We had literally just launched it when they closed down all the hotels, and we didn't know what to do," recalls Hannah.

It was their management company that came up with the idea of renting the hotel to the local council during lockdown to accommodate homeless people. The authority agreed a rent of £7,300 a month which left Hannah and Gwyn with a profit of £3,500.

They also had control of a four-bedroom house in Cardiff under a rent-to-rent agreement which was let out to construction workers and was making £1,500 to £2,000 per month before the Covid crisis.

Now their sights are set on far bigger ventures. They have clinched a lease option agreement on a derelict building and are applying for planning permission to split it into 21 flats. If approved, the projected margin will be £1.2m to £1.6m.

Hannah is clear about her reason for going into property.

"I wanted freedom to live my life how I want to. I didn't want to be stuck in the rat race, getting up at five in the morning, coming home at eight and hating my job. I had to make it work and I love what I do now."

Samuel says: "Hannah's gone from having no savings to achieving financial freedom just from one deal alone. Where she's got to since coming on the crash course is rare. She's a perfect case study. If someone said to me pick the top ten people you would choose to do a joint venture with, she'd be one of them. If anyone has the opportunity to do business with her, do it because she really knows her stuff, works hard and has a lot of integrity."

HANNAH'S TIPS

"You can always find money somewhere if a deal is good enough."

"I learnt so much from networking and talking to people who are in property and doing well. You need supportive people around you."

"My investment from my personal portfolio is going into cryptocurrencies and stocks because it's turning over really good money. I don't just want to keep it in the company. I like to invest it in different things."

Chapter 9 – John Raybould

Sheffield university student becomes a 'property mogul' in between his studies

Most students would never dream they could be financially free by the time they graduate, but that became the reality for John Raybould after he set up a property business in between his full-time studies.

John was in his third year at Sheffield University, reading history and politics, when he had a lightbulb moment after he realised that, like the landlord of his digs, he could be making money from renting out rooms.

By the time he left university John co-owned four houses with his father which were generating around £4,000 a month in rent. It was enough to cover the 21-year-old's bills. He then went on to add four more properties to their portfolio. It includes six houses in multiple occupation and two single lets.

John, from Ecclesfield, began his journey to financial freedom after being inspired by Samuel Leeds' book, *Buy Low Rent High.*

"I remember I was in my student house reading the book and it suddenly struck me that myself and four friends are all in the same house paying rent on rooms. I'm thinking that's adding up to quite a good deal. I was getting quite jealous of the landlord! That enlightened me and propelled me into the idea of making money from renting. I thought why wait till I leave university to get started."

John decided he needed to gain expertise and enrolled on Samuel Leeds' Property Investors Crash Course in 2018. He then joined his training academy which gave him the advanced skills and knowledge he needed to source successful buy-to-lets.

Before attending the crash course, he had already set up his property firm, Raybould Properties Limited, and persuaded his father, also called John, to become a director. A quantity surveyor in the building trade, he had started to dabble in property himself.

His father had been intent on doing up houses and then selling them on for profit, having previously bought a terraced house to refurbish and a plot of land next to it to build a new house. He had also purchased another five-bedroom property at auction to renovate and sell on just before his son joined the academy.

"My dad was initially sceptical about the crash course and the direction I was going in. I managed to change his vision completely and convinced him that the return on investment would be greater with a rental strategy – and that if we kept these houses they could also go up in value."

John then used his newly acquired skills to scour the country for more good investments. He located two properties in Burnley and Gainsborough which they converted to create a total of ten rooms. John did all the spadework, negotiating the best buy-to-let mortgage deals.

They bought the Gainsborough house for £112,000 and it is now giving them a monthly profit of £1,100. The four-bed Burnley house is being rented out for £1,400 a month. In total John estimates the profit from all their investments at between £5,000 and £6,000 a month. The figure fluctuates as not all his rooms are occupied all the time.

"My dad had an interest in development projects and also had equity in his house which he could use. We work well together and it's strengthened our relationship. He's been very supportive but, if he hadn't come on board, I would have found another venture partner. You have to show persistence."

At an initial one-on-one session, Samuel advised John how to approach potential investors over the telephone for funding. Within half an hour John had secured £400,000 from family and friends to start him off on his property journey after he put some of his student loan in as a deposit to join the academy. He has since attended 15 Property Investors Crash Courses to pick up more tips and help others hoping to make money from the housing market.

Along the road he has experienced problems with some benefit tenants not paying their rent and being badly behaved. His solution was to install CCTV in communal areas. To his horror he saw some visitors were smashing chairs in the kitchen. They were subsequently prosecuted for criminal damage.

If any tenant on Universal Credit does not pay their first month's rent, he now applies to have it paid directly to him by the council. John has also had to contend with the discovery of Japanese knotweed, an invasive plant, in the garden of one of his other houses. It cost him £5,000 to treat.

"I've had plenty of problems, but I view them as challenges, and you get over challenges. If you want to be wealthy you can't stop at problems. You've got to get over them."

Samuel said: "For such a young guy, who was still at uni when he started out, John has done incredibly well. He's got these properties going up in value and cash flow coming in which he will be saving to put into other houses to generate more passive income."

John says his friends do not fully understand what he is doing but one said: 'I hear you're a property mogul.' "I'm trying to build my own brand. I want to set up a secure future for myself. Although university is a path a lot of people go down and then get a job, I'm doing things differently now.

"I want my dad to be financially secure as well and to be able to leave his job if he wants to. He's 55 and has given me a lot in life, so I want to help him massively."

He added: "Without the training and support from Samuel Leeds and his coaches, I wouldn't have been able to get into property and know how to deal with the problems I've had. I've also met lots of people on the academy and other networking events. It's important to have a circle of people you can talk to about property issues and resolve them together as a team."

Now aged 23, his short-term strategy is to acquire more HMOs and cater specifically for benefit tenants. He says it is a good business model because there are not many landlords doing this, and there are clear advantages. The houses are cheaper to buy and require only functional fittings, as opposed to the high-end finish demanded by tenants in professional jobs. He can also get the rent paid directly into his bank account, giving him good cash flow.

John's resilience has not just been put to the test in his property dealings. Soon after meeting Samuel, he accompanied him and his brother Russell, CEO of Property Investors, on a charity mission to Uganda with several other successful academy students.

While there in July 2018, they were taking part in a team-building, white water rafting experience on the River Nile when their boat capsized.

"We went over a waterfall. I feared for my life at that moment. There was a plunge pool below and I got sucked down into it, even though I had a life vest on. I was quite deep under so I couldn't get back up very easily but when I came up from the plunge pool, I was pulled into a rescue boat straightaway. Some people were dragged quite far down."

John escaped with bruising and cuts, but his mentor smashed his kneecap and lost a lot of blood. He had an operation and spent 10 days in hospital. On his return home doctors told him he might never walk properly again and is still suffering the effects.

Despite this, John says Samuel gave them all a rousing speech from his hospital bed and persuaded them to carry on with the purpose of the trip, which was to identify villages in need of fresh water wells.

Both the Leeds brothers are committed Christians who give 10 per cent of their profits to charity and have carried out extensive work in Africa to improve the living conditions of impoverished people. John hopes to follow their example when he has enough cash flow. In the meantime, he is enjoying been hands-on with his business, contacting estate agents daily to find more deals.

He talks every day to letting agents as well to make sure the rents are coming in and all the houses in his portfolio are maintained. If any renovation is being carried out, he also liaises with the team to check on progress.

"I could pay someone to manage the properties and take the profit, but I would stagnate as person. I'm just wanting to grow my business as fast as I can which is why I'm hands-on."

"Use the resources and people around you to your advantage. My dad bought a small development project at the end of my first year at uni. So when I went into property investing, I brought him on board and it's working well.

Some people might say it was alright for me because my dad had equity in his house which I could use, but you have to show incredible persistence to start with."

"Develop a mindset that says any issues you encounter are not problems, but challenges which can be overcome. Some young would-be property entrepreneurs might have a fear of talking to estate agents and be worried they might not be taken seriously because of their age. They might see that as a problem. If you view it as a challenge, it's easier to overcome. If you view it as a problem, you can have a mind block and can't do it."

Chapter 10 – Callum Mathieson

20-year-old turns mum's legacy into the gift of financial freedom

University student Callum Mathieson used some of his inheritance from his mother who died from a brain tumour to help himself become financially free and raise funds for patient support groups.

Callum Mathieson said 'his whole world was shaken' when his mum Lorraine succumbed to glioblastoma multiforme (GBM), a particularly aggressive type of cancer. He was determined, however, to make the most of her legacy and now earns thousands of pounds a month as a property investor.

The Oxford Brookes student was surfing the internet while working nights in a petrol station during the summer holidays when he spotted a YouTube video by Samuel Leeds on investment strategies in the housing market.

Six months later and the 20-year-old had control of five rental properties which give him enough cash to live on and pay his bills, despite the fact he owns none of them.

Callum even has enough money coming in each month to save his student loan and has just entered into a joint venture to buy a block of flats which will also be rented out.

The second-year economics, finance and international business student spent £10,000 of his mother's £60,000 bequest on advanced training in how to gain high returns from property. It equipped him with the skills to negotiate 'no money down' deals which allow him to rent out accommodation without being the legal owner. As part of the contract, he gives the landlord a guaranteed monthly rent and pays for all the maintenance and cleaning. He then lets it out at a higher rate and keeps the difference.

Callum, from Sutton Valence, near Maidstone in Kent, has attended several free Property Investors Crash Courses run by Samuel. The undergraduate also enrolled on the company's paid-for academy, confident he would recoup the money through having the knowledge to invest properly.

He secured his first deal after posting a string of messages on Gumtree seeking potential 'rent-to-rent' partners. One reply was from a Japanese landlady who was out of the UK eight months of the year and needed someone to manage the rental of her one-bedroom flat.

After viewing it with a fellow investor, they agreed to take it on as a furnished apartment for short stays. Then it emerged she also had a five-bedroom house in Oxford which she wanted managing.

Callum and his partner initially considered renting it as a single let but then realised they could increase their income tenfold if they turned that property into serviced accommodation too.

The landlady paid them to install en suites in two of the rooms and they now let all the rooms to visitors to the city.

Callum said: "We worked out we were probably going to get £85 a night on average per room. So, instead of £500 net profit a month each, it's more like £5,000 net profit a month.

"If those two properties are both occupied at 75 per cent, it works out at about £3,000 net profit for me."

Since signing the contracts for these two properties, he has secured three more rent-to-rent deals on two apartments and a penthouse in a new block of flats under construction five minutes from Ascot Racecourse in Berkshire – with a different joint venture partner. Callum met him while attending a *Deal Finding Extravaganza* event organised by Property Investors.

In addition to this deal, Callum and five other academy members are hoping to secure a bridging loan to buy 12 flats in Scarborough and then pull out some of the money to invest in other projects. Callum now also runs his own property sourcing firm and is transitioning into property development.

He said a big reason for becoming a property investor was to turn his late mother's money into a lasting legacy.

"She was an accident and emergency nurse and worked long hours. When the inheritance came through and I started seeing it shrinking away, I didn't like that. I was thinking my mum hasn't left me this money to waste it on bills or go on holiday.

"I've always liked property and interiors. I love watching *Million Dollar Listing* (a reality TV show about selling high-end properties in American cities). After she died, in 2018, I tried to buy a flat in Oxford for £250,000, but the mortgage broker told me to come back when I was 21 because I had no income. I was looking to borrow 25 per cent of the cost. It was just as well I was refused because it would have used up all my inheritance. Factoring in the legal costs, my return on investment would have been four per cent which is also much lower than what I get now.

"It was only when I found out about the rent-to-rent strategy that I realised property could help make me financially free. As well as raising funds for patients recovering from GBM, I want to set up a charity which does research into the disease."

One of his two elder sisters is also hoping to follow in his footsteps and get the same training after being impressed with his progress.

Samuel Leeds, chairman of Property Investors, said: "I started out in property at 16 with no money and I was a multi-millionaire before I was 30, so there's no reason why a 20-year-old can't make it with the right education and drive. I'm really impressed with what Callum has achieved in such a short time. There are so many opportunities out there and seeing him make the most of them and networking so well is very satisfying for me. I always say that anybody can become financially free and carve out their own life."

CALLUM'S TIPS

"I attended my first Property Investors Crash Course in London in July 2019. Then I went on a launchpad course to learn specifically about the rent-to-rent strategy, how to find a deal and lead and how to contact people.

"I've been to two more Property Investors Crash Courses since because of the opportunities they provide for networking and meeting trades people and potential joint venture partners. The last two crash courses I went to were in Birmingham. I picked up different lessons at each one of them and I love the energy that you get from them. I've also been on a course about sourcing and selling property deals to investors.

"That would be my tip. Get the right training, so that you know what you're talking about when you approach estate agents and landlords – and keep refreshing your knowledge. It gives you a kick if you find yourself slowing down as I did after my first two deals."

"The academy has also been very good for me, particularly the Mastermind group of six people who, like me, are interested in doing rent-to-rent deals.

"I went with a member of the Mastermind group to the viewings for my first two deals. He used to run an assisted care business providing housing for the disabled. He knows a lot about refurbishing properties. I thought he's going to provide a much better quality of property than I would. He suggested joint venturing and I said, yes let's do it. It's a good idea to partner with someone who complements your skills."

Chapter 11 – Rahim Bah

Foster child from war-torn country in Africa who grew up to become a property entrepreneur

Property entrepreneur Rahim Bah grew up in war-torn Sierra Leone and moved on his own to England when he was just 15.

Rahim grew up in London in a crime-ridden neighbourhood and could easily have strayed from the straight and narrow. His foster mother, however, was determined to help him succeed and he too avoided the gangs that roamed the streets of Croydon where he lived.

He studied hard, first at college and then at Bournemouth University, graduating with a degree in accountancy and finance. Then he landed a job as an accountant in the capital.

But when his firm relocated to Brussels Rahim decided he wanted to stay in the UK and moved to Cardiff where he believed he could achieve his potential, away from the distraction of family and friends in London.

On a salary of around £30,000 a year life was good, but he was looking for a different direction.

"I enjoyed accountancy at the start but then it became boring. I didn't like to be told what to do. I just wanted to be independent.

"I always had a desire to go into property but thought all the time you need lots of money to do that and I didn't have that."

One day he was searching the internet for general information about property when he saw a video by Samuel Leeds and then ordered his book, *Buy Low Rent High.*

"I bought the audio book and listened to it over and over again. It helped me greatly, especially the emphasis on how to secure a no money down deal. I memorised it and watched all Samuel's other videos on YouTube.

"At first I thought Samuel was too good to be true to be honest but then I realised what he is doing is actually real."

Rahim attended one of his free, two-day Property Investors Crash Courses in September 2018 and at the event found six deals.

Four were rent-to-rent agreements and two buy-to-lets. He used the cash flow from his rental properties to put down a deposit on one of the houses and a bridging loan to purchase the other one.

"It was a no money down deal basically. The only money I put in was the refurbishment cost. They were both fully licensed for five years as HMOs in Cardiff, so I didn't even have to get licences.

"Within two months of going on the course I was financially free and making a residual income of about £7,000 a month."

Aged 27, Rahim quit his job soon afterwards. Two years on and he is running a company in Cardiff, dealing in property sales, lettings and management. Rahim now has a manager who oversees his estate agency as he now focuses mainly in renovation and development projects as well as his own training company to share his knowledge and experience.

"I learnt from the crash course that no matter who you are, if you're hardworking and have been guided, you can do what you want to do in life. It's all on you. I believe in working hard and then your luck will follow.

"After the crash course I worked twice as hard just to see if I could get these deals and then it happened. At the beginning I thought how do I get into property with no money? But then I watched Samuel's videos and knew what to do. I knew he was there as an example of what you can achieve. It gave me confidence."

Rahim added: "When I was in school and they had parent meetings, I had to have my foster family come, rather than my real family. It was one of my lowest points but at the same time it motivated me because they were there for me.

"I do still call my parents from time to time and I still speak to my foster mum of course. She brought me up in a way that I could do well. She was absolutely amazed when I told her what I was doing and is so delighted and happy to have been part of my life."

Looking forward, he wants to return to Africa with Samuel Leeds to help with some of his charity work. That was one of his other reasons for wanting to become financially free.

"I was a youth ambassador in Croydon and I believe in giving back to the community."

Samuel said: "Rahim is an amazing person. He's done so well. Going from foster care to university is a massive achievement and then to become financially free in two months is incredible."

RAHIM'S TIPS

"The best advice I can give is find people like Samuel to guide you and get you to where you want to be. I believe if I'd had him in my life sooner, I would have achieved so much more. Since I've met him it has accelerated my business and he's helped me systemise it.

"I cannot thank him enough because, if I hadn't met him, I wouldn't have had the motivation and the hunger to move on."

"Find people that have already done it. Then copy them."

Chapter 12 – Katy Lai

Airline employee sees her property profits soar after acquiring new knowledge from Property Investors

Airline employee Katy Lai has been a landlady for more than 20 years, earning a side living from renting out houses after renovating them. However, it was only when she attended Samuel Leeds' training programmes that she truly learnt how to be a successful investor.

Katy became interested in property after reading Robert Kiyosaki's bestseller, *Rich Dad Poor Dad,* which encourages people to concentrate their efforts on buying income-generating assets.

She came across it by accident while on holiday abroad. "The only English book there was *Rich Dad Poor Dad*. I thought it was going to be a story book but actually it changed my life."

That was in 1998 and slowly over the following years she built up a portfolio of six buy-to-lets, using the BRR strategy (Buy, Refurbish, Refinance).

"At the time I didn't know it was called that. I just thought this was a good way of increasing the value of the house and then refinancing it. I kept doing that and then, when I had any equity spare, I would invest in another property."

The monthly profit from the six properties was around £2,000, but Katy was put off making more investments when the Government made two key changes affecting the buy-to-let market. It introduced a three per cent stamp duty surcharge on additional properties in 2016 and then brought in new Section 24 rules the next year, reducing the amount of tax relief landlords could claim for mortgage interest payments and other finance costs. The aim was to discourage competition between property investors and first-time buyers.

"When Section 24 came in, no one seemed to know what was going on or what the tax was going to be. Because I didn't have enough knowledge, I actually stopped investing in property. I got scared," said Katy who lives in Northamptonshire.

The solution came when the mother-of-three watched one of Samuel's YouTube videos explaining how to overcome Section 24.

"I was like wow, this is amazing, why didn't I see this before. My properties were all single lets and, whilst they were making me about £2,000 a month, they were under threat because of Section 24. After watching that video I binge-watched all of Samuel's other videos."

Katy then tried to get a ticket for one of his free two-day crash courses, but it was over-subscribed. Undaunted, she posted an appeal on Property Investors' Facebook page, asking if anyone had a spare ticket.

"Luckily a man messaged me and offered me one for free. His sister couldn't make it. He met me outside the venue for the crash course and we went inside together. It was just meant to be."

Soon afterwards she joined the Property Investors' Academy to acquire an in-depth understanding of strategies for building wealth through the housing market.

Between watching Samuel's video about Section 24 and attending the crash course, Katy had also refinanced all her properties and released the equity. She then went house hunting and found a two-bed property in Leicester which she bought for £151,000.

Initially she had planned to turn it into a four-bed HMO but then discovered there was an Article 4 direction in the area, restricting change of use of a property.

"It was an error but then again you are always going to encounter problems and brick walls. As long as you try to find a solution, I think at the end of the day you'll be fine."

Her confidence paid off. By the time the sale went through it was worth a minimum of £190,000. She found an international scholar employed by the university and another scholar who rented the house.

"They paid the top dollar for the whole year. That lump sum has helped me with other projects.'

Since attending the crash course and joining the academy Katy has bought four more properties in the same area. Three are being rented out and the fourth one is about to go on the market.

All four will generate about £3,000 a month. She is paying a monthly fee for the furniture for the next three years. "It means I don't have to shell out for furniture, and I save on tax. Once that's paid, I will be making a profit of £4,000 a month."

She solved the Section 24 problem by buying the properties through a limited company which she set up, calling it KCM after the initials of her children, Kirsty, Chloe and Matthew. Interest can be declared as expenditure if you buy through a company.

Her fourth house cost her £126,000. She put down a deposit of £40,000 raised from one of her other schemes. Katy took out a bridging loan to pay for the rest. The £60,000 refurbishment was also funded through bridging finance. She expects the house will be worth over £200,000 once the renovation is finished. After refinancing she anticipates leaving in £20,000 to £30,000. En suites were added to each of the four rooms to increase the rental yield.

Katy has an HMO manager whom she met while viewing potential investment properties. She manages 15 rooms for Katy and charges eight per cent of the monthly rent collected.

Despite her success, the 42-year-old has no plans to leave her job which she loves.

"I work with a brilliant company. It was something I always wanted to do. Property is also something I always wanted to do and being a good mum. I feel quite blessed. Things happen for a reason. If you look for good things, good things will happen, so I try to have that sort of mentality."

She added: "The reason I wanted to go to another level in property investing was to leave my children a legacy. I want to show them that no matter what it is you want to do, as long as you try, you learn and use the knowledge you can succeed. I want to be a role model for them. They're my inspiration."

In future she plans to take on more BRR ventures and house 'flips' with the help of angel investors so that she can provide people with good living conditions.

Samuel Leeds said: "Katy is a really positive person. She has great energy and a presence about her. She provides a high standard of accommodation and I'm sure she will continue to be an inspiring role model for her children."

KATY'S TIPS

"You need to get out of your comfort zone. I'm really shy in front of camera so I'm recording myself talking to camera and posting it on social media. I find that difficult, but you have to get comfortable doing the uncomfortable. That's one of the rules you learn on the crash course."

"If you want to become a property investor just go for it. Get yourself educated and once you're educated implement that knowledge. Don't give up. As long as you keep going you will succeed. The more you do it, the easier it becomes.

"If it wasn't for what Samuel Leeds offers, for example the free crash course and free videos, I don't think I would be where I am today. I wouldn't have that knowledge. I wouldn't be able to progress further. I would still be behind the brick wall, just sitting there not progressing or learning. Because of what I learned from his videos and courses it inspired me to learn more and do more.

"I loved going through the training programmes. I loved the energy, the atmosphere, the community. If there was something that I wasn't sure of, I would ask on the Facebook page, in the groups or approach the trainers directly.

"Each programme had its own benefits. The *Deal Finding Extravaganza* was very good. I may do deal sourcing in future because I do come across a lot of good deals. I can't take them all and sometimes I've offered deals to friends and family for free. I didn't realise deal sourcing is a business. It might not be passive income, but it is massive."

"Education is very important. How you take that education and implement it is also another factor. You can go through lots of problems and make errors, but it will be cheaper if you get it right in the first place."

"You can have your job, but I think it's very important to have a passive income so that in the unlikely event something happens you have enough to secure yourself. That is why I went into HMOs because of the good cash flow you can get."

Chapter 13 – Stella Samuel

Gamble pays off for IT analyst after taking out a £20,000 loan to buy an eight-bed HMO

Most people can only dream of being able to go to work each day out of choice rather than necessity. For IT employee Stella Samuel, however, it is a reality she is still getting used to. If she was suddenly fired or handed in her resignation, she would have no financial worries.

What gives her this freedom is that she has built up an income as a successful property entrepreneur after enrolling on the Property Investors Crash Course and then the academy.

At the age of just 28, Stella is making a monthly profit of between £3,000 and £4,000 from renting out short and long-term accommodation which she does not even own. And the application analyst, from London, is still doing the day job because she wants it that way.

Stella started out in spectacular style after attending the crash course in October 2019 and signing up for the academy on the same day, using her savings of around £10,000.

She then took out a bank loan for £20,000 to pay three months' rent, plus the deposit, on an eight-bedroom HMO in Oxford. Having persuaded the landlord to furnish it, she went on to re-rent it at a higher rate. It took her just three weeks to let out all the rooms, with six of the rooms each having a separate en suite. The owner was happy to receive a guaranteed rent every month and Stella welcomed the cash flow.

That property rented out so quickly, she was able to save the profits and recycle the loan into securing more rent-to-rent agreements, all of which were legally drawn up. Stella recalls finding Rent-to-Rent houses live at

Samuel's training programmes. During the breakout sessions she would phone up the owners and managed to secure deals straight from these Academy events.

In total, she controls four HMOs, all in Oxford, and a one-bedroom serviced accommodation property in London.

Stella admits she took a big risk, but the training with Property Investors, she says, gave her the knowledge and confidence to take it on.

"It was a massive commitment. I knew I had to make it work. I had a bit of fear, but I had to put it to one side because I knew this was something I wanted to go into. I had to make sure the numbers worked, and I had the right training to go into such a deal.

"That first deal took a lot of hard work. I got a lot of 'no's' before I got that one. I was basically just knocking on doors, speaking to people and waiting for that yes. It was daunting going through that process but once I'd got that yes it was just amazing. I got the house through an agent. It was beautiful."

Her SA in London is renting out well. She obtained that one directly from the landlord, sealing the deal in a week. Most of her bookings come from Booking.com as well as Airbnb and HomeAway. In the first month of it going live in January 2020, the property was booked for 50 per cent of the days available, rising to 80 per cent two months later, she said.

The training received in the academy has been key to her making money, in particular the Rent-to-Rent Revolution course, which is helping her to systemise her business. She has also benefited from the three-day *Deal Finding Extravaganza* course and Infinite Returns module about the Buy, Refurbish and Refinance strategy.

"It was amazing. I got so many good nuggets of information from that. You can't just do the crash course and look at Samuel's YouTube videos. You've got to be in the room. You get more information out of it. You get your questions answered directly. You're sitting with people who want to learn like you. You can bounce ideas off each other. It's a fantastic place to network as well."

Three of the HMOs Stella runs are owned by relatives. She took on two of them before the crash course after deciding to give property a try because she was unhappy in her job.

She looked at YouTube videos, researched the subject and joined property groups before becoming a member of the Property Investors' Academy programme. She also watched Samuel's popular Winners on a Wednesday interviews with his high-flying students, little thinking that she would one day be featured herself.

"I'm still in shock that I've been on a Winners on a Wednesday video. I never would have imagined that I would come this far."

Her family was initially sceptical about her property dealings but now both her mother and aunt are in the academy.

"At first they thought I was crazy to go into rent-to-rent. They'd never heard of that and said it can't work, but as I took on the properties, they saw it was actually working and possible. Now they call me for advice."

From having a side business, alongside her job, she is fully focused on property these days and plans to move into BRR projects.

"Samuel's enthusiasm in making property a business really resonated with me instead of seeing it as a side business. I'm going out there talking to vendors as if it's my business. Having that attitude has changed the way I'm speaking to people. They take me more seriously and are now coming to me with offers.

"I'm still in IT in a nine to five job but it is out of choice. It's easy to say now I'm financially free I can move. I need to get in the mindset of leaving that traditional route. I'm still working on that but I'm almost there."

Samuel Leeds said: "Stella has done brilliantly because she has done her due diligence, done the training, spoken to the right people and put in the work to get to where wants to be. The next level is for her to become a property investor and find the right BRR deal.

"She asked me if I had any properties that I wanted her to rent. I love that! That's what you need to do sometimes in business. You need to ask the question. She will definitely be in my top black book of people I'll reach out to when I have an opportunity."

STELLA'S TIPS

"Dreams can come true if you put in that effort and keep on striving for what you want to achieve. It will happen. It's not just for the one per cent. It can happen for you."

"Make sure the property you find is in the right area. Make sure the numbers are correct. Don't go into a deal just because there's a deal on the table. Make sure it's a good deal. A lot of people will throw bad deals at you and you will probably be tempted to sign one of them because you want that first deal but actually hold back. Make sure it's correct and take that time to consider it."

"Go on the crash course. The people are friendly and willing to help you out and you can network."

Chapter 14 – Piers Bishwakarma

Property income gave entrepreneur freedom to be with sick father in hospital when he needed support

It is a nightmare scenario. Your father becomes seriously ill and is admitted into intensive care. You have a decision to make. You either stay with him in hospital to support him and risk losing your job over your enforced absence – or you prioritise your work.

That is precisely what happened to Piers Bishwakarma when his father Gopal, an ex-Gurkha captain, contracted meningitis. Luckily, Piers was not faced with this Hobson's choice. As a successful property entrepreneur, he was able to be at his dad's side for a month while he recovered.

His passive income from renting out furnished apartments was more than enough to cover all his bills without the need to go out to work.

At the age of 28, Piers is his own boss and while he sat from 6am to 10pm maintaining a bedside vigil he planned his next business move on his laptop.

"I had a serviced accommodation business, but I was just sitting there with dad, spending time with him trying for him to get back into a normal life.

"At that point I was thinking what's next for me. My dad and I used to talk and then I did some work. That's when I clicked with myself and thought, actually, I'm sitting here doing pretty much nothing and I should be making the most of this time."

As a member of the Property Investors Academy, Piers had learnt in detail how to source and package profitable housing deals and pass them on to investors for a fee.

That is when he hit on the idea of setting up a bespoke investor club.

"I looked at what was in the market already and how I could be different. I was getting a lot of people saying to me, because of my success with my serviced apartments business, I want to start too. They were asking me how to find a deal.

"That's when I started deal sourcing but rather than just finding deals and putting them to an investor list, I decided to walk people through the setup and actually show them the business of serviced accommodation – as opposed to simply saying here's the deal and these are the numbers."

It has proved a winning formula. In 2019, he made around £30,000 from sourcing on top of his rental income of between £25,000 and £30,000.

However, it has not all been a smooth ride since Piers attended the Property Investors Crash Course in October 2018.

He used the knowledge gained from the crash course and Property Investors Academy programme, which he completed in November 2019, to negotiate a rent-to-rent agreement on four flats in an apartment block near the town centre. In exchange for giving the landlord a guaranteed monthly rent, he was allowed to re-let them at a higher rate.

Piers and his older brother Mahesh, an engineer, invested £8,000 of their family money in furnishing two one-bedroom and two three-bedroom flats, and had to pay the first month's rent of £3,600 on top. It worked well for a while. Bookings came in through Airbnb and booking.com from business travellers and construction workers building new homes in Aldershot who needed somewhere to stay.

But after a year, the owner exercised a legal break clause allowing him to take back control of the apartments and rent them out himself. In one fell swoop, Piers was £3,000 a month down in his business account.

Since then he has bounced back, replacing the block of four flats with three rent-to-rent deals on serviced apartments, which give him an average income of £2,500 a month.

"I did feel I'd been used as a guinea pig when it happened, but from a business perspective I just said to myself things like this happen in business and I've got a chance to move on. I've no regrets.

"I was lucky that I managed to find apartments run by landlords who had given up on them. I found the properties through Gumtree and OpenRent. I took them on and made them work.

"A lot of landlords have given up because stock levels of SAs are going up but if you know how to operate them you can still do well."

Piers moved with his family to Aldershot, the home of the British Army, in 2008 from Nepal. His father worked for the army for 25 years before retiring in September 2019.

Before becoming a full-time property entrepreneur, Piers was a partner in an Aldershot estate agency helping ex-Gurkhas settle in the UK. Previous to that he was also a store manager for a mobile phone firm and a retail franchise owner. He took up his new career after hearing about Property Investors' chairman Samuel Leeds and discovering he was a self-made multi-millionaire who was the same age as him.

"I'd been thinking about property investing for some time. I watched all of Samuel's YouTube videos, then enrolled on his crash course, along with my brother who has supported me on my business journey."

Piers' story was published in his local newspaper, the *Aldershot News and Mail*, which led to a property developer in the area offering him £100,000 to invest in a joint venture project with him.

However, he turned it down, having just pulled out of a separate joint venture.

"It would have allowed me to scale my business up to big numbers last year, but I thought if I get someone's £100,000 investment how do I put that into a relationship for the next five to ten years. It's not just about the money. It's about the relationship, and how both people can add value to it as well."

Now he says he is ready again to enter into a joint venture. "I'd like to joint venture with a landlord of a block of apartments to run a serviced accommodation business. I still want to run my SA business as successfully as I can too – and give people the opportunity of understanding how to run one and be able to tap into my knowledge to get good deals. The biggest challenge is for me to form a joint venture and scale up the business."

Piers says if it was not for his property income, he would have been unable to spend so long in hospital with his father. During that time, they bonded in a way they had never had time for before because they were both so busy at work.

To celebrate his father's recovery and retirement, he surprised him and his mother Shilu with a business class flight to Nepal. "They had a blast. To be able to do that for parents that just felt good. I never thought I'd be doing that when I started out. I'm happy and I'm liking what I'm doing."

Samuel Leeds said: "Piers has branded himself really well. He's also found his own niche in deal sourcing. To make as much as he is from packaging deals and his rental income is the dream. What he's got going for him is his heart and spirit which is to see people succeed. He had a positive rippling effect throughout the academy when he was with us and has done really well."

PIERS' TIPS

"If you like Samuel's videos, just go on the crash course straight away. I wasted seven months before I went on the course."

"Use your knowledge to action things quickly. Don't think I still need a bit more knowledge. For example, if you want to run an SA business but don't have a deal yet, think about how to get that deal first. If it's just picking up the phone to agents, do it."

"If you really want to do something and you see there's potential in it, think about the three and five years ahead that you want to see yourself in. If it ticks off both the boxes, take action."

"We've been taught in the academy to give value, so I did a free Google my business for serviced apartments video. I posted it on a serviced accommodation network, and I had over £2,000 views, all organic, and people commenting. Always look to add value in some way."

"Be open to learning. If it means finding a mentor and paying them to train you in a short space of time, do it. Samuel has been an inspiration for me. To learn about the steps that he's taken to becoming successful has been amazing."

"If you want to start sourcing properties for investors, learn about the process first, then co-source with someone initially. Do it for free. You'll find a deal on behalf of a legal sourcer who already has a client database. Stack it up in terms of calculating the return on investment and work with that sourcer. They can stack it again and send it to their clients. That's how you are going to build trust."

"Have fun. That's what I did in 2019. I had loads of fun. I was in Nepal for 27 days for my cousin's wedding and had a blast with family. It's all about balancing it out."

Chapter 15 – Kellie and Shanelle Edwards

Couple who spent their wedding money on property training become successful rent-to-renters

They had it all planned, a lavish wedding ceremony to cement their relationship of five years. However, the day before the last payment was due Kellie and Shanelle joined Property Investors' Academy, using the money they had saved for their big day and have never looked back since.

The couple took out a bank loan instead to get married, officially becoming Mrs and Mrs Edwards, and put on ice the celebration which would have cost them thousands of pounds.

Their decision paid off. By investing their savings in training to become property investors they became financially free within six months.

It was a huge turnaround in their fortunes after years of hard graft, working up to 60 hours a week in a variety of low-paid jobs, including delivering pizzas. At one point they did not see their family and friends for three months because they had no time to themselves.

Now Kellie, 24, and Shanelle, 25, could stay at home all day long if they wished and still have enough money coming in to cover their bills, thanks to their passive income from rents.

The pair signed up for the academy on the final day of attending one of Property Investors' hugely popular crash courses. After completing the Rent-to-Rent Revolution module, their eyes were opened to the possibility of earning a living from property without actually having to invest in bricks and mortar.

They went on to secure four rent-to-rent deals with two developers of new apartments after learning on the course how to explain the benefits to them. As part of a legal agreement, they pay the landlords a fixed, monthly rent and are allowed to re-let the accommodation at a profit. The rent was free for the first three months with no deposit to pay and a management company handles the bookings for them on sites like Airbnb and Booking.com. In total, they can host up to 14 people.

Three of the properties are in an apartment block in Cardiff, within an easy commute of the seaside resort of Barry, where they live, and the other one is in another flat complex in Swansea. As an added bonus, Kellie has been able to employ her brother, who had been homeless, as a cleaner.

Their outlay to date has been £4,000 which they spent on furniture. Depending on the time of year and demand from short-stay visitors, the average rental income per month is £2,400.

With plans to take on a further two flats, which would give them control of the whole block in Cardiff, as well as a penthouse in the city, this figure is set to rise substantially.

Shanelle says it is the perfect arrangement. "We learnt from attending a deal selling masterclass as well that once you get in with developers and promise them guaranteed rent it's a win-win situation for you and them because they don't want hassle or maintenance."

Kellie says she still feels like she is in a dream and never thought they could be successful business people who would be financially free so soon.

"The crash course was held on the last weekend of July 2019 and we had to make the final payment for the wedding on the Monday. That was the only money we had, but we thought if we don't join the academy now, we'll never do it. We'll figure it out when we get home.

"Our attitude was, we don't need to have a huge wedding. We love each other. Why waste that money? So, we just had a little wedding and invested in property."

Both agree it was worth it. "We thought when we make it, then we can get married again and have a big wedding celebration," said Shanelle.

It was in Australia that she first became aware of the potential of business to transform their lives after travelling there with Kellie to find better paid employment.

"They had crazy wages over there, double what you get here for the minimum wage. I was working long hours in a restaurant, loving the money. But then all these people would come in and spend just as much as I was earning every week eating out. I asked them what they did, and they said they were investors. They had time to do whatever they wanted in this amazing country, so I thought I need to learn how to get a passive income."

When they returned home after a year, Shanelle began looking into making money from the housing market and quickly came across Samuel Leeds and his training company. Again, they found themselves working long hours for poor rewards which fuelled her desire to find a more lucrative living.

"We thought the life we wanted to live wasn't matching up to what we were doing, and something needed to change. We would wake up at 6.30, leave the house at 7.30 and wouldn't be home till 11.30 at night because we were going from one job to another. There was no way we could maintain this for another 40 to 50 years."

Shanelle had an additional motivation for succeeding in business. A month before going on the crash course, she had an operation for an ovarian condition, similar to the one which had claimed her mother's life.

"I was 13 and an only child when my mum died. Everything that I ever knew in life, where we lived, where we rented, was all just gone. So that's burning inside me to make sure I don't leave my children early and with nothing."

They believe their property business has brought them closer as well since they got married in August 2019.

"We lean on each other a lot," says Shanelle. "We blend well because Kellie shoots off all the emails and gets speaking to the landlords. I'm the one who insists all the figures have to be right."

It is easy for some new investors, she adds, to fall at the first hurdle. "From attending the crash course to securing deals and seeing money coming in is tough because you don't know what direction you want to go in. That's the window where some people will give up.

"I never felt like giving up but it was like, come on when is this going to happen? It took us about three months to find our direction. We knew we wanted to start acquiring assets, but we weren't in a position to do that, so we needed cash flow. We targeted rent-to-rent because we didn't have much money to start with. Now we're moving on to acquiring assets.

"Kellie has a disabled cousin, so we're looking into the assisted living sector because in Barry we know there's a shortage of suitable properties. One aspect of our business is going to be HMOs for vulnerable people and adjusting them for their needs. It's a bit of BRR (buy, refurbish, refinance) and combining strategies."

They also intend to set up cleaning and maintenance companies which will feed into their serviced accommodation business to keep everything in-house.

Samuel Leeds said: "They're a power couple who have different levels of skill to offer people and they're very energised. They believe in themselves and the training. It's great that they're also using their business to bring self-employment to one of their family members who was really in need. Their success is my oxygen."

KELLIE AND SHANELLE'S TIPS

Kellie: "Without training we wouldn't here doing what we're doing. At the crash course we sat there with our jaws to the floor listening to the speakers. We keep going to more crash courses. It's almost like a drug now. I'd recommend doing that. We learn more each time and get to network with people which is so important.

"The academy has also been fantastic. We've learnt how to speak to landlords and negotiate deals. Property Investors also helped us set up our website."

Shanelle: "You have to step back from your life and what you've got going on because it can just consume you. You're not thinking about your future, you're just trying to get through one day a time."

"My aunty said to me at a family event, 'oh I thought you'd turn up in a yellow three-wheeler, Dell Boy. I've also has been told don't change, but as Samuel says, the whole point is you want to change when you go into property investing."

"We've been on stage at one Property Investors event to talk about what we've achieved, and it was scary, but it's good to get comfortable feeling uncomfortable. You always get nervous doing something new. We're enjoying every step of the way."

"It's like a family being on the academy. The people we've met are incredible. We're all in this together to make our lives better and we're all trying to help each other on that path to financial freedom. The knowledge we've been given has been outstanding."

Chapter 16 – Zayyan Farran Armani

Graduate earns £5,000 a month from rent-to-rent deals two years after leaving university

Like many 18-year-olds, Zayyan Farran Armani was unsure what he wanted to do with his life when he left school. So, in common with many of his peers, he followed the university route, even though it would saddle him with a debt of more than £40,000.

He won a place at Aston University in Birmingham to study business management and public policy and was enjoying his course. In time, however, he became aware that if he wanted to become wealthy his path to success lay elsewhere.

As Zayyan put it: "I became interested in personal development and then realised university might not be the main way for me to learn. I asked myself whether I should be learning from lecturers who aren't millionaires, or from people who were in a position where I wanted to be."

That thought cemented his future actions. He finished his degree and landed himself a well-paid sales job with a software company. Then he started to pay his mother's rent.

"I thought that's £500 a month. How am I going to pay for that? I don't want to pay for it out of my own pocket, so I decided to go into business."

Searching on YouTube for ideas, he came across Samuel Leeds and watched one of his videos on lease option agreements. Over the coming months, he viewed all of Samuel's content.

Armed with this knowledge alone, the sales representative managed to negotiate a rent-to-rent deal, with a six-month break clause, on a one-bedroom apartment in Reading where he lives.

"A friend introduced me to the landlord after I let it be known that I wanted to go into property investing. He was struggling to let it because the rent was too high. I took a chance on it because the flat isn't in a central location."

Despite this, he broke even in the first month after spending £2,500 on new furniture, including a sofa bed for the lounge.

Zayyan pays the owner a guaranteed £825 a month. In return, he is allowed to rent it out as serviced accommodation to businesspeople and visitors needing a place to stay for the night.

He took the apartment on in July 2018 and in that first month made a profit of £1,500 – three times his initial target to cover his mum's rent.

Now the 26-year-old earns £500 to £1,300 a month from bookings through Airbnb and Booking.com

Since then he has gone on to secure two more rent-to-rent deals consisting of another one-bedroom apartment and a four-bed HMO in Bracknell and Windsor.

In total, his passive income adds up to about £5,000 a month which is enough to make him financially free.

Zayyan quit his job in June 2019, just two years after leaving university. The following November he attended his first Property Investors Crash Course.

Having been hugely motivated by Samuel's YouTube videos, seeing him in action live impressed him even more.

"Samuel is awesome on YouTube but when he gets to the crash course, he brings some fire. He's got real energy and such a positive vibe. The information he gives you is amazing and it's free."

Zayyan has gone on to do advanced paid-for training with Property Investors which has given him the confidence to expand his portfolio. He spends a part of each day relaxing in a spa and sauna where he often makes new business contacts and also goes networking.

As a full-time property investor, Zayyan employs his mother in his business to help him with jobs. She is his biggest reason for going into property, he says.

"My parents split up when I was five. My mum worked crazily for me and my two sisters when we were growing up. She had it tough, but she's also been strong. She's a real entrepreneur herself. She opened up a post office and put us through private school for some periods and also got two properties during this time. I really appreciate what she's done for us. How I turned out is largely due to her.

"Ultimately my 'why' is to pay off the mortgages for her houses and pay for anything my sisters want. My younger sister is now at university. I want to get her a property too so she can stay in it and start renting out rooms."

He also gets his 'fuel' from people in his past who doubted him and accused him of having no goals in life, he says. "I've got to make sure these guys don't get the satisfaction to ever think they were right. That motivates me."

Samuel Leeds said: "Zayyan's story is remarkable. For a 26-year-old who has left university only recently to be financially free is a big deal. He now has an enviable lifestyle which other people with the right training and work ethic could achieve."

ZAYYAN'S TIPS

"Get your website set up, get knowledge and get your contracts in place. Those are for me the key things you need. As long as you've got those, then you should have enough confidence to go out there and show your product."

"Sometimes you work better with a stranger than someone you've known a long time. It's really important not to close yourself off to people or not network or pick up a phone. Speak to as many people as you can about what you do and go to places where you can meet other people in business. You never know where that can lead you."

"If you want to be a property investor, go for it and invest in yourself. People fly in from China to attend the two-day Property Investors Crash Course. They're investing in themselves. What else are you going to do during those hours to change your life?"

"Both serviced accommodation and HMOs have their stresses. You get jittery if you haven't had a booking for a couple days with an SA. I know from experience I will get bookings, but now I'm not just relying on Airbnb and Booking.com. I'm trying to build relationships with other agencies finding accommodation for corporate employees or remote workers flying in from somewhere like America for a week."

"With an HMO there's a lot of groundwork involved, but once you get people renting it out it's a lot more passive than having to turn over an SA. If you want a consistent cash flow, then an HMO is a good strategy. That's why I combined it with serviced accommodation."

Chapter 17 – Ruaraidh Macleod

Samuel Leeds' videos help millionaire businessman to branch out into property developing

As inspirational stories go, Ruaraidh Macleod has a compelling tale to tell about his journey in life. Ruaraidh came from a broken home and conquered a drink and drug addiction to establish the UK's biggest guttering business with an £8m turnover. He discovered the Church of Scientology along the way and has also branched out into property developing after watching Samuel Leeds' YouTube videos. His life, however, could so easily have taken a downward turn.

The entrepreneur learned about business early in life through necessity. When Ruaraidh was 9, his parents split up and due to his mother being on benefits and having very little money he was forced to get a job by the age of 12 working for a newsagent's in the village of Duntocher in Scotland.

The youngster got paid 75p an hour to deliver newspapers and worked in the evenings and on Sundays to build up a paper round. Soon he was making £30 a week.

"In those days, that was a fortune. That was the money I used to live on – well, more to fund my extracurricular activities – but I did learn about having to work hard to make money," he recalls.

"Even on the paper round, which was quite large, I had to do some basic administration, like keeping a log of who paid what and counting my money. I also had to buy the newspapers. I made a profit and that was the money for the papers the next week.

"My business brain was beginning to form at that age. It was more out of necessity than anything else. Other children got pocket money from their parents and I suppose I resented them because they would use that to get a drink at the weekend, whereas I had to work for my money.

"Now I look back and realise it was a gift from God because I really learned at a very young age how you make money."

Samuel too had a paper round as a working class boy growing up in the West Midlands. He says most of the people he knows who have become extremely wealthy through business also delivered newspapers as a child.

"People think when you are rich you were born wealthy but actually there are a lot of people out there who were born into poverty and have become rich because they had to learn about business."

Ruaraidh worked hard to make a success of himself but he also looked for escapism. While still at primary school, he was offered a spliff. It coincided with his parents separating and his mother also experiencing severe mental health issues.

"I remember smoking it and feeling elated and 'out of it' which for me was a nice experience because at the time it was a bit rough at home."

He experienced the same sensation with drinking. "I had my first drink when I was 12 as well. I had three bottles of cider with a friend. We would go out and get drunk and then I just started doing that every weekend. That's when I would sit in my room, play my computer, work and go and get drunk and take drugs."

Despite his difficult start in life, Ruaraidh managed to get to art school and also gain a business degree. But it did not help him to achieve his dreams. His first job after leaving university was in a call centre earning £12,000 a year, selling car insurance and commuting two hours a day by car.

His life was unsatisfactory in other ways. He longed to have a relationship with a woman but felt too inhibited to form one. Help came from the Church of Scientology, which gave him the tools he needed to improve his situation, he says.

After going on a detox, which cleaned him up physically, Ruaraidh enrolled on some practical business courses. As a result of this training, he set up a stair cleaning business in Edinburgh.

"I had a real stigma about doing it because I had a degree, and here I was mopping and cleaning stairs. But I quickly saw that I could grow the business and actually make a lot of money doing it which I did. I got to the point where I was making in a day what most people were making in a week."

The young businessman saw his contracts shoot up quickly from eight to 50 using the principles he had learnt through Scientology.

He met his future wife through the church, as well as his business partner, Stuart Guy.

Scientology has had very mixed reviews over the years, but Ruaraidh says it helped him to turn around his life at a time when he felt broken and lost.

"All Scientology is and has ever been is something that gives you really effective tools which you can use in your life. It helped me with communication and business, and I make no secret of my passion for it."

The 42-year-old describes his four years at university as a 'complete waste of time.' He used to sleep through the lectures and whenever he picked up a book, he would nod off.

"The main reason why I went was to get the grants and student loans to fund partying and going on holiday, but there wasn't a lot of information absorbed. I just didn't know how to study or how to learn."

By contrast, he found Samuel Leeds' online video content, highly engaging.

Ruaraidh had seen at an early age how money could be made in the housing market. His father, who was a teacher, bought properties below market value, doing them up and then selling them for a profit.

"My dad had bought and sold about seven houses by the time I was nine. We moved a lot, and I saw how he was making money through property."

Ruaraidh also experienced both sides of the social divide growing up. He lived just outside Glasgow in Clydebank, a predominantly working class area, and in Bearsden, a more affluent neighbourhood.

Property came to the fore again when his business partner Stuart introduced him to Samuel's YouTube videos in 2018 and they started watching them together.

"What Samuel does is he will show you a real-life example of a house and explain in detail the different ways you can buy it. There's so much information there for someone who doesn't know about buying or renting a property and the content is very well laid out. You're given lots of examples – he shows pictures and films which help you understand more about a subject than just the written word.

"It's so different to university, where somebody's got a set hour to talk and you have to listen and try to piece it all together," says Ruaraidh.

With the knowledge he and Stuart had gained, they bought a barn with land for £450,000, using some of their own money and a bridging loan. They originally agreed to pay £500,000 but renegotiated after having it valued at £450,000 and finding out there was Japanese knotweed on the site. They spent around £60,000 on renovating the barn for domestic use and now rent that out, along with a commercial barn in the grounds. The site is now worth in the region of £700,000, but they don't plan to sell it any time soon as it is producing a healthy rental income.

Together Stuart and Ruaraidh own six commercial properties. Ruaraidh has also bought a bungalow in West Sussex, where he now lives, after driving past it one day and noticing its large plot. It had two bedrooms and three reception rooms, as well as a huge back garden. He saw the potential to create a four-bed property and purchased it for £350,000.

The businessman then put £100,000 into extending the rear of the bungalow and giving it a makeover inside and out. The improvements included a new bathroom suite, large patio doors, a smart-looking driveway and landscaped gardens. The plumbing and electrics were also replaced. He then moved in and had it revalued at £550,000, giving him a profit on paper of £100,000.

If he sells the bungalow, he will not have to pay any capital gains tax because the property is his primary residence.

Ruaraidh owns the house he is living in for business reasons, but like Samuel agrees that it is best to rent your home to avoid tying up your own money.

"I've always rented properties over the last 10 years. The main upset I have with owning your own house is you have to have a large chunk of cash sitting in it. When I say sitting in it it's not true. The large chunk of cash goes to the bank which uses your money to make more money, so I'm better off taking that money and investing it myself."

This is why, even though his business, Bens Gutters Limited, is doubling in size every year and turning over millions, he never has much cash in the bank.

"I never really hold cash. Generally, I will borrow money to do things like this. If you can borrow money to do a deal, which gives you a profit, you then get cash flowing back once the debt is repaid. If you just slam your £200,000 into a property, then it limits what you can do."

Samuel Leeds agrees with this thinking, actively teaching people the advantages of renting where they live if they are a property entrepreneur. Samuel himself lives in a rented house to free up cash for investments.

"A very wealthy friend said to me if you've got millions of pounds in the bank, you're probably a bad businessman because if you're a good businessman how could you sit with millions in the bank?

"I know when I've got a lot of money in the bank it irks me. You want to leave a little bit in because you never know when you might need it. If you've got staff, you need to be responsible but generally speaking it's not good practice to be some kind of hoarder of money," says Samuel.

He approves of the way Ruaraidh went about developing his bungalow. "Most people, especially when they're living in a property, will spend £30,000 say on putting in a conservatory, but they'll only push the value of the house up by the same amount, so it's completely pointless.

"Ruaraidh spent £100,000, which sounds like a lot, but he pushed the value up by £200,000 and made a £100,000 tax free profit. That's being commercially savvy.

On a personal level, Samuel says it makes him feel fulfilled to know that his videos and other material that he places online are benefiting people financially.

"I've also learned a lot from Ruaraidh about business and personal development and I'm really honoured that I've been able to play a part in his journey on the property side."

RUARAIDH'S TIPS

"Having an employee or a business partner is like having a wife. To find someone you trust, look at the whole person. For instance, if they talk negatively about others, ask yourself why you're going to be any different. If they're unfaithful to their partner, why will they be faithful to you? It's important to look at their track record as well and get referrals. I use a recruitment company to get my senior managers."

"Establish your goals and write them down. Tell someone you trust about your dreams. The more you look at your objectives and talk about them, the better your chances are of achieving them."

"Walk away if the deal doesn't quite stack up. I did that with a large property development. I was unhappy with the return compared to the work it would involve."

"Education is about gaining knowledge for use. There's no point in going to university if you don't know why you're learning a particular subject. If you want to be the owner of a big construction company, get a job in construction and work your way up."

Chapter 18 – Joshua Sarai

Academy 'prodigy' negotiates two house deals before his 18th birthday

Joshua Sarai has a lot in common with Samuel Leeds. They both started out in property investing in similar ways, negotiating their first deal when they were just 17. Their families gave them a helping hand at the outset and they never let their youth be a barrier to success.

Both were also adamant that they never wanted to go to university and have instead applied themselves tirelessly to studying business, taking their inspiration from great entrepreneurs.

Samuel was delighted to welcome Joshua into the Property Investors Academy, seeing himself in the younger man in many ways, and has given him valuable advice from the beginning of his journey.

It was Samuel, who taught him how to find a creative solution to the problem of getting onto the property ladder when you have no money and cannot get a mortgage because you are too young.

Still only 18, Joshua became a full-time property entrepreneur after only eight months of training and has proved himself to be a real asset to the academy and his family.

He picked up the keys to his first house for the equivalent price of 'a good meal out' and is well on the path to building up a whole collection of them to hang from his key ring.

For as long as he can remember Joshua has wanted to be a businessman. He read Robert Kiyosaki's best-selling personal finance book, *Rich Dad Poor Dad*, when he was 14 and has been studying how leading business figures made their wealth ever since.

But the teenager from Milton Keynes had to overcome a few obstacles en route to becoming a fully-fledged investor. First Joshua had to persuade his parents to put him through the Property Investors Academy instead of university.

"I always wanted to be in business. I knew wholeheartedly that was the way to go, but I got really serious when I read Robert Kiyosaki's book," he says. "I was very inspired by that, so I started watching all these people like Grant Cardone, Dan Pena and Kiyosaki. I also read about very successful businesspeople from the past like Andrew Carnegie, Rockefeller and Ford. It put me in a state of mind that it can be done."

After Joshua sat his GCSEs, a family friend drove him to his prom in his Lamborghini. It was at that point that Joshua realised that if he wanted to be rich, he had to work for it.

"I remember it was the summer holiday and I was sitting in that car thinking I need to work now. After that I went full steam ahead and haven't stopped since."

Having researched the American property industry, the budding entrepreneur searched Google for information on how to invest in the UK housing market.

Samuel Leeds' YouTube videos came up straight away, he recalls. "I remember Samuel just shouting down the camera: 'this is what you've got to do.' I thought he's got the most energy, I've got to follow him. I binge-watched all of his videos and took notes.

"I wanted to meet Samuel and get into property. I was really driven to do it."

Still only sixteen, Joshua concluded that he needed to be 21 to be an investor and set up an online drop shipping business instead. However, he pulled the plug on it after a while because all he could think about was property.

That was when he discovered there were strategies he could pursue in spite of his youth, such as a buy, refurbish, refinance and rent project with a guarantor or packaging up an investment deal through a co-sourcer.

"I realised that to grow rich you need to dig deeper. You don't just pack up and go home. You need to look further and think creatively to find that success, and that's exactly what happened."

Joshua first had to overcome a major hurdle before he could fulfil his ambitions. Both of his sisters had gone to university and had very good jobs. His parents thought he should do the same.

"My sisters are both very successful, but I knew their route wasn't for me. They were the first to say let him do it, when I was showing my parents about property investing, and saying it could be done even at my age."

Joshua's mother Rani admits she only went along to one of Samuel's seminars to 'shut up' her son.

"He dragged me along after going on about property and Samuel for ages, but then I had to apologise to Joshua because he had me sold on it immediately."

Now he only had to convince his father, so he brought him along to a Property Investors Crash Course. He was impressed by the positive environment and realised it was possible for Joshua to become successful with training.

The family invested a few thousand pounds in sending Joshua and his mum on the *Deal Finding Extravaganza*, an advanced training programme where they learnt how to put a power team together and book lots of viewings for a 'big day out.'

After attending the DFE, Joshua got his wish to meet Samuel who spoke to them about the Property Investors Academy.

"Samuel didn't pressure-sell us at all. He gave us time to think about it," said Joshua.

However, he and his mum soon saw how they could benefit from the network of people with different skills which the academy would introduce them to and both enrolled.

Armed with knowledge, Joshua did his market research and found a house for sale in Hull through RightMove. It was on the market for £45,000 and needed work doing on it. Aged just 17, he put in an offer of £39,995, just below the Stamp Duty Land Tax threshold of £40,000, and it was accepted by the motivated seller.

On Samuel's advice, he decided to find a joint venture partner. His parents were the natural choice. They put in the money and pulled most of it out. The legal fees amounted to £984 plus £350 for a survey and £7,485 for the refurbishment, bringing the total cost to £48,830. The new value of the property was £65,000.

After refinancing it with 75 per cent loan-to-value, it meant they had only effectively put £63 into the deal.

As Joshua puts it: "It was the price of a good dinner."

The interest payments on the mortgage amount to £97 a month which will be more than covered by the rent. The house has been on the market for a fortnight (August 2020) and is already attracting a lot of interest.

Monthly rental values range from £425 to £475 in the area and Joshua is confident they will achieve the top figure due to the standard of the renovation carried out. This will leave them a profit of around £300 after costs.

Samuel says Joshua's first deal demonstrates how you can get started in property investing with no funds. "Even if you haven't got the money to buy the house you've found, or can't get a mortgage, if you can find good deals, everything else will just follow. You can raise the money, enter into a joint venture, or package and sell the deal to somebody.

"If you can become valuable, no matter how old you are, and can find good deals, the money or the investors will just come. This is something I teach."

The young businessman pulled off another coup when he found a property on RightMove, again in Hull. It was a six-bedroom, turnkey house share, which meant that it needed no work doing, and it was already being rented out at £350 per room, yielding a gross profit of £2,100.

Joshua negotiated the asking price down from £155,000 to £138,000, found a letting agent and then passed it to another deal sourcer who was a fellow Property Investors Academy member. The co-sourcer sold the deal to an investor for £3,500, paying Joshua a £1,200 fee. The investor ended up pulling out and Joshua was gutted, but he ended up finding his own investor and sold it himself for the full £3,500.

His goal now is to source one deal a week. He has already begun to build his own list of investors, having created a website to attract business. He also hopes to complete more BRRR projects with his family.

Joshua is full of praise for the Property Investors Academy. "The academy gives you all the knowledge and skills you need to be a successful property entrepreneur. It saves you five to 10 years of mistakes and rejections. If there's something you don't understand, the academy will answer that for you.

"The network and ability to communicate with trainers like Samuel Leeds are also so valuable and you can find joint venture partners. Each person in the Property Investors Academy has an individual skill that can benefit you and you have a skill that can benefit them.

"Some people are surveyors, for example, some people know builders, and some are accountants. You might not have a power team but if you communicate with people you can potentially have a full-on power team. We found builders through another academy member.

The support from webinars and calls during the lockdown has been a great plus too, he says.

"I've seen other people being active and thought I need to do something, otherwise I'm just wasting three to four months.

"Even if you don't catch any deals, you can use this time for reading. I've been reading books on property investing for the entire lockdown."

But he warns success doesn't get handed to you on a plate. Hard work and persistence are vital.

"The academy costs £10,000 which is a lot of money, especially to an 18-year-old but that's not your ticket to the riches. You're not going to join the academy and six months later a Rolls-Royce appears outside your front door. What you put in you get out. I viewed 15 houses before I got my first deal."

He is also indebted to his parents for their faith in him. "No money can ever repay that. They really do believe in me and what can be done. It's allowing me to give them what they want as well – the things they've worked so hard for."

Samuel is also grateful to a family member for having trust in him when he was a fresh-faced youth, barely out of school. When Samuel found his first investment property, his stepfather Tim put the mortgage in his name and the rest, as they say, is history. Hundreds of deals later, Samuel owns a large portfolio of properties and a training company in Property Investors which has taught thousands of ordinary people how to gain financial independence through investing in the housing market. Samuel still has that first house, never having wanted to let it go. The mortgage payments were easily covered by renting out the terraced house in Bournville, Birmingham after he converted a sitting room to turn it into a four-bed property. In fact it has made him a rental profit of £100,000 - and it has doubled in value since he bought it during a recession in 2009.

Similarly, Joshua has no intention of selling his first house. "I wouldn't want to give it away. It's like my baby. Wherever I am in 10 or 20 years, I'll always remember that was my first deal and look at what it's created."

JOSHUA'S TIPS

"Know how to discover an opportunity and just get yourself on the racetrack to capitalise on it. Your success starts with a thought. Once you find that thought try to create a plan and then execute it."

"We live in a country that people lose their lives trying to get to. Don't waste that opportunity. This little island we're on is already one opportunity, so take full advantage of it."

"The hardest thing has been trying to understand that 'no' is good. The more no's you get the closer you are to a yes!"

"If you're refurbishing a property, keep a close eye on your builders and communicate with them. I set up a WhatsApp group with our ones."

"If you're serious about becoming a property investor and don't just want to make £1-2,000 a month, then take the training because it's worth more than the price tag. One of the biggest mistakes you can make at my age is taking financial risk and messing up. Get professional help."

"Try to surround yourself with like-minded people who are in the same industry as you and speak to them. You might have a piece of advice for them too."

"You might think there is some sort of secret structure or an algorithm to how to conduct business. There isn't. It's simply about doing and not thinking or caring what other people think."

"Our house was the greyest house you could imagine, but by finding the worst properties you're benefiting yourself. You're building your portfolio and bringing good houses to the market."

"If you want to get someone in on your vision, show them what can be done and that it can be done. Then give them time to understand everything and eventually they will say yes."

"The secret to making a million is not just 'here's a million, here's how you do it.' You have to figure it out yourself. If you are ready for this, it will show itself to you."

Chapter 19 – Deborah Hey-Smith

Samuel Leeds repays his former teacher's faith in him by giving her life-changing lessons in property investing

Property Investors' founder Samuel Leeds and Deborah Hey-Smith owe a huge debt of gratitude to each other. She was his teacher who encouraged and believed in him, despite the fact he was always getting into trouble at his Christian school.

Mrs Hey-Smith, as Samuel still calls her, taught him the key skills he needed to make his way in life and ultimately to become a millionaire property entrepreneur.

Years later, Samuel repaid the favour when he taught her how to invest wisely in the housing market after she was made redundant. As a result, she now has a full-time income from property.

Their connection is deep-seated. Mrs Hey-Smith has been present at some of the most important moments in Samuel Leeds' life. She can remember him when he was knee-high to a grasshopper, coming into school with his brother and sister, and his mother who was a teaching assistant in her class.

Mrs Hey-Smith gave him lessons in maths, IT and typing, while her husband taught him history. She witnessed the highs and lows of his school life.

"I wouldn't say he was the star pupil," she admits. Samuel laughs at the memory.

"I was on the verge of being expelled. I was suspended regularly. I had probably the most detentions than anybody in the school apart from one other person."

Mrs Hey-Smith saw beyond all of this, focussing instead on the potential she saw in her pupil.

"When I was a child myself I used to play around a lot at school and get comments on my school reports which I didn't find very helpful. I thought I never want to be a teacher who gives negativity out to the children. I want to be always positive, encourage them, and see what worth they've got because I believe everybody has a God-given skill.

"Samuel was very good at communicating. That was his gift and I think that comes through now in his crash courses. He's quite quick at thinking on his feet as well."

During a typing lesson she remembers he was asked to write about a biblical character and he naturally chose his namesake. In Clipart, he added an enormous ear and a quote from the Bible which said: 'God, I'm listening.'

"I thought Samuel as a person wasn't listening to God, so I kept it on the wall for about two years.

Then one day he was sitting in front of it typing away with ten fingers and I just got the word evangelist.

"I thought that is your calling, to be an evangelist. I feel now he is an evangelist – not in the conventional way but in a different way through property."

Samuel agrees. "They call me the financial evangelist. Although I teach property, I'm very vocal about faith and the meaning to life."

After leaving school at 16, he wasted no time in taking his first steps as a property entrepreneur. Within a year he had bought his first investment house in Bournville, Birmingham. His stepfather, encouraged by the early signs of Samuel's clear business acumen, agreed to have the mortgage put in his name.

Samuel reconnected with his one-time teacher when he set up Training Kings, a Christian business networking group which eventually had branches all over the country.

Mrs Hey-Smith came to the first Training Kings event in January 2014. She enjoyed it so much that she went on to become one of the leaders at the Birmingham group.

At Training Kings, she noticed a difference in Samuel who was 'starting to develop as a confident, outgoing person.'

"The skills which God had given him were being developed. I was very impressed with him and gave him a testimonial," she says.

She also gained a glimpse of Samuel's future as it was through Training Kings that he started teaching people about property investing.

Deborah Hey-Smith later travelled to Africa with the Property Investors founder and his wife Amanda, on one of his first charity missions there. She and her husband accompanied the couple to Zambia where they were providing a well in a village.

Samuel recalls his former teacher making an important intervention. He says she hurried along the builders after they initially struck a dry borehole. The water came up a week after they left.

Mrs Hey-Smith's overriding memory is of seeing the children's excitement and giving them their cups to collect the water in when it arrived.

She was with Samuel again at the first ever Property Investors Crash Course. After inheriting her mother's house in the Yorkshire countryside, she started to think like a property investor herself.

Her first taste of property investing turned out to be on a grand scale. Doing up the old and dilapidated house would incur VAT. Instead, using a loan from a relative, a builder was employed to demolish it and construct three five-bedroom houses on the land. There was no VAT to pay and the houses were then sold – and the loan repaid.

At the crash course Mrs Hey-Smith learnt about all the different strategies available to investors to make money in the housing market. She was able to capitalise on a chance investment while in Bangor, North Wales, for her daughter's university graduation day.

She saw an estate agency advertising a house which would make 'a great investment.' The word investment sprung out at her and she arranged a viewing.

"I remembered what Samuel had said about asking for a lower price. I didn't mention that at the viewing. I just said to the owner I think this would make a great house for students. It was in a good location, in walking distance of the station and the university. I thought I could do it up as an HMO."

She made a 'ridiculously low' offer of £80,000 on the £110,000 asking price. As she expected, it was rejected. However, the owner made a counteroffer of £95,000 which she was happy to accept.

The estate agent recommended a builder who installed gas, new walls, fire doors, smoke alarms, central heating and double glazing. The refurbishment cost £5,000 and she simply put a bed in the sitting room to create a third bedroom.

Mrs Hey-Smith now makes a profit of more than £1,000 a month from renting the house to students. She also refinanced the property which, following the improvements, was valued at £130,000. It meant she was able to pull out about £90,000. She took out some money to give her only daughter Abigail a wedding to remember.

She also used a further £45,000 from refinancing the house to expand her portfolio. This time her target was a property in Stockton-on-Tees in County Durham. She put £25,000 towards the £70,000 purchase price and is now renting it out to a family, boosting her income by another £575 a month.

A visit to Sheffield to pick up a car from her sister's house also resulted in another significant acquisition. This time she bought two unfurnished houses, with her sister joint venturing on one of them.

Like Samuel, Mrs Hey-Smith believes that financial education is 'so important.' She says children should be taught about money at school – and even study subjects such as property investing and joint ventures.

She believes the school curriculum should be radically changed. "I would re-write it. I think a lot of it is a total waste of time. It doesn't actually give the children what they need in life and I think that's what schooling should be about, giving them the financial education.

"I was blessed to be in a school where I was able to teach people to type with ten fingers because why teach people to write with a pencil when people were using typing?

"A lot of things like typing are not taught in school. It's a fundamental thing, maybe not now so much, but you should be able to use a mobile phone with both your thumbs. Most children can, but I don't know how to use a mobile phone most effectively."

Samuel can type fast and expects people who come for job interviews to be able to do the same – and know how to manage money, depending on their role.

"When I was in Uganda in 2019, we negotiated with the government to build a school. I said I'll pay for the school as long as you let me come in and teach money. I think it's just basic."

Teaching youngsters how to generate a passive income which in future will keep coming in even when they are 'sleeping' is also important, says Mrs Hey-Smith.

She is now 63, and for her, a steady cash flow is vital as she was made redundant and has not yet reached the state pension age.

"Property is great for generating a residual income. Now I can live off my rental income. I have to as I'm not old enough to have my pension because they keep changing the age.

"My daughter has just been told her pensionable age is going to be when she's 75. Who wants to be working till then? Some jobs you can't physically do when you're that age.

"If I hadn't had a rental income, I would have signed on for Universal Credit and might have applied for some teaching jobs. Because of the competition, I might not have got a job and then I would have resigned myself to being on benefit for the next ten years or so. Then you just go down a spiral hole because there's nothing to really motivate you. Having property has been great and I love it."

Samuel is full of praise for his one-time teacher. He says she wants to encourage other people because 'that is her heart.' She proved him right when she met a 74-year-old woman who was a landlady. She invited Mrs Hey-Smith to view her house and after a while, due to some problems with renovation work, she agreed to manage the project for her.

Having done some research, she concluded that in the condition the property was in, it would sell at auction for £40,000. Once it was refurbished, she believed the value would be at least £130,000, given the prices of other houses in the area. She chose a builder after checking out the quality of his previous work.

The cost will be around £50,000 which includes replacing all the windows, replastering and redecorating the rooms and fitting a new shower. Once finished there will also be two toilets, with a bathroom, kitchen, lounge, three bedrooms and a garden.

Mrs Hey-Smith wanted to supervise the project as a favour but the landlady offered her a gift of money for the time and effort she would need to put in and so she accepted that.

Samuel describes her as a soft, caring person but wonders how that fits in with the hard approach needed to get a good deal. Her reply is that she comes from Yorkshire where they 'talk straight' and she is not afraid of being direct when she needs to be. "I always believe never pay full price for anything."

Mrs Hey-Smith is also frank in her views on how the media has treated her ex-pupil. She has seen him come under the spotlight over allegations of his training company pressure-selling – something he has always denied strenuously.

She says: "I think very much in this country we have a culture where we build somebody up and when they get to the top, we tear them down. We saw that with people like Princess Diana and Meghan Markle recently.

"I think we have a very bad media. The BBC was built on Christian principles, but those principles have just gone out of the window in my opinion. It's the same with schools. A lot of the Christian principles, even that the whole country is built on, people just disregard.

"Bad publicity does hurt, but you just have to look at the positives. You've got to be true to yourself, to know what you're doing you believe to be truthful and right and get on with it."

Looking back on Samuel's journey, Mrs Hey-Smith says she is pleased how her ex-pupil has demonstrated his belief in himself and expanded his operation. There were seven people in the room at the first Property Investors Crash Course. When returning for a second time, she was amazed to see the audience had swollen to around 1,000. She particularly appreciated the chance to work in small teams while also networking.

She adds: "There've been so many people on the property courses who've come out and said things like... oh I've got a property portfolio worth £1m in four or five years. It's just incredible what Samuel's teaching's done."

Looking to the future, Mrs Hey-Smith is considering branching out into deal sourcing as a strategy. "I think I'm quite good at getting good deals on properties and getting quite high but fair rentals. I would like to help other people get properties where they could become financially free.

"I'm also hoping my daughter and son-in-law will eventually get some properties of their own, so they have an extra income."

She is also interested in providing serviced accommodation in Birmingham because none of her existing properties are in the city. "I think it is an up and coming place for young professionals and also people who just want to come for short breaks. It's a destination where not a lot of people go to at the moment. I never wanted to live or go to Birmingham because it was a no-go area. I feel it's still got a very bad reputation outside Birmingham. But there's a lot going on for a short break and the Commonwealth Games are coming too. There is an opportunity in this sector to do really well."

Samuel says: "I really appreciate that Mrs Hey-Smith has been there from the start. Every time I've started a new business or initiative, she's been there. She'd be one of the people I'd call if I was ever in trouble.

"She's definitely encouraged me, not just today, but for the last 20 odd years, which has given me the strength to go and encourage people through my training courses and my YouTube videos which get millions of views.

"I'm grateful for her support and so pleased to have been able to teach her about property. She's a great negotiator and good at getting things done, and cheaply. She's bought properties in the right areas and they are all going up in price nicely.

"Even if you inherit some money and live off it, it can shrink and turn to nothing. If you invest it into something that's going to give you an income, then it's forever."

MRS HEY-SMITH'S TIPS

"You have to self-educate and be open to change. I had an inheritance but there are strategies to get involved with no or little money which you can learn more about on advanced Property Investors courses."

"Think about your future, especially if you're young. Where are you going to get that money from if your pension age is 75? Property can give you a residual income."

"I get returns of 10 per cent plus on my houses through rent. If I put that money in the bank, the interest can be as low as 0.1 per cent. I also like to say that property doubles in value every 10 years. It's a win-win situation."

Chapter 20 – Pastor Clement Okusi

Church leader who once doubted Samuel Leeds sees his property income shoot up by £10,000 a month

In America they give you a round of applause when you are doing well, but in Britain they look at you suspiciously and say, 'what have you done wrong?' That is the opinion of Pastor Clement Okusi who is a property investor when he is not engaged in his church work.

He has seen the income from his portfolio shoot up by £10,000 a month since attending the Property Investors Crash Course.

And yet he found himself amongst the doubters when negative reports appeared on the internet and in the media about Property Investors' founder Samuel Leeds. He even joined an anti-Samuel Leeds Facebook group.

It was Samuel who showed Clement how a simple change of strategy could transform his earnings from property and, before long, his monthly profits had risen sixfold.

The senior pastor bought his first house in 1996, the year he got married, after seeing how his brother had made a lot of money from property investing.

The house in Lewisham, South London cost £60,000 and he rented out the rooms. Two years later he sold it for £112,500.

"The tenants had to sort out the bills amongst themselves and whatever they did they shared it amongst themselves. That covered the cost of the mortgage and put money in my pocket on top, plus it gave me a profit of over £50,000 for doing nothing. I couldn't believe it," says Clement.

For several years he worked in the City of London for a merchant bank and acquired several more rental properties which provided him with a steady, if not spectacular income.

They were all single lets as he had decided letting out the rooms individually would take up too much of his time, especially when he entered the ministry.

Then in 2018, the full-time pastor attended the Property Investors Crash Course after watching most, if not all of Samuel Leeds' videos on YouTube.

Clement had already been considering trying to make money from HMOs, but after Samuel explained the strategy at the course, he decided it was a 'no-brainer.'

"It made complete sense. I was sitting there thinking, why didn't I do this years ago?"

One of his properties was let out on a single tenancy to three men who had brought in two friends to share the accommodation.

"Effectively, they were HMO-ing amongst themselves in my house. I wasn't bothered by that. They paid their rent, on time, but at the end of the tenancy I told them I was going to transition to renting out the rooms individually."

They wanted to stay and agreed to pay him £500 each and slightly more for the larger rooms. In one fell swoop, the rent he received went up from £1,400 a month to £2,650 just by altering the way the rooms were let out.

Samuel shared another valuable tip in one of his YouTube videos which made a huge difference.

"I remember Samuel saying you turn a front room into a bedroom by putting a bed in it. It felt like that was too easy, but it is as simple as that."

It was a pleasant surprise that the changeover from single to multi-lets also consumed far less of his time than he had anticipated.

"There's actually very little difference between the two. I was nervous it was going to take me more time to manage, but if I spend two or three hours a week on my portfolio that's a busy week – for example if someone's broken a washing machine and I've had to get involved.

"It's been safer as well. I had a single let where the tenant didn't pay the bill. I've never had an HMO tenant not pay their bills. Even if they did, at least you've got other income streams coming in from that property. When you have a single let and they don't pay their rent, you're not getting anything from that property."

He points out that there are other advantages too, one of these being that a landlord is legally entitled to go into the property to do checks and maintenance if it is a multi-let. This is not the case if it is a single let.

With the exception of his first house, Clement has focused his investing activities on Croydon in South London. All of his properties are located within a 15-minute drive of where he lives and are rented out to working professionals.

"I have had one or two graduate students but mainly they are people who work a job with a regular income. I offer them very nice, newly refurbished, clean modern accommodation at the cheapest price. Very rarely are you going to be able to rent something like this cheaper than what I'm offering."

He is proud of his own achievements "When I went on the Property Investors Crash Course, I was making £1,000 to £2,000 across my portfolio. Now I'm making £10,000 to £12,000 profit per month through property, just by changing my strategy."

As well as having HMOs, Clement has added another strand to his investing. He buys 'tired' properties, especially targeting those which only need a light refurbishment. He does them up to increase the value and then refinances the mortgages. He says he has already done two such projects in 2019 and three so far in 2020, while in the future he plans to carry out developments.

Entrepreneurs are more made than born, Clement believes. Environment is also a key factor in fostering a spirit of enterprise, he says.

"I was born to Nigerian parents and they by nurture are entrepreneurs. They might not be the best ones, but they've certainly got an entrepreneurial spirit about them. In some cultures, entrepreneurship is just a way of surviving because there is no welfare system or government assistances. So, if you don't work out how to turn a pound into two pounds you're going to be stuck.

"I believe anyone can be an entrepreneur if they can acquire the mindset of an entrepreneur."

Clement's mother died when he was young, and he and his four brothers were raised by his father in a council house. "It was a very alpha male but poor environment. It's interesting, though, that none of us are poor today. It has to do with this upbringing and nurturing.

"Even then, when you get something you are always very aware what it's like not to have anything.

"Sometimes when you come from a poor background you like to hang onto it because you don't want to go back to where you've come from. If you want to be an entrepreneur, something has to shift in your mind – that you've got the skills, the knowledge and the belief so that even if you were to lose, you'd get it back again. Having said that, I've never lost a property."

As a grandfather, Clement's primary motivation for investing in property is to leave a legacy for his children and their children, but growing up poor also drove him on to succeed.

"I know what it's like to be poor and not to be poor. Which would you prefer? There's so much difference, but also so many of our problems in our community are economic. Parents are working two or three jobs trying to make ends meet. The kids from poor backgrounds typically tend to get in trouble.

"Money doesn't make you happy, but money does allow you to make choices that can take away some pressures which can give you a sense of happiness.

"I was raised on welfare in a single parent home. I left school in 1988 and every month since I've left school someone has given me a pay cheque, alongside me being an entrepreneur. For me Britain is such a great nation. It's a land of milk and honey and great opportunity. Anyone with any gumption and some energy owes it to themself to do well."

He says the man who washes his car is an example of someone who came to this country, in this case from Eastern Europe, and worked hard to make a success of himself.

"He's washing cars seven days a week. I don't envy him. He works when it's cold and snowing, but he owns a fleet of vehicles and houses and drives a Range Rover. In fact, the last time I saw him he was at an auction buying properties. He's employing people and doing well for himself. So, I don't think you've got any excuse to be poor in Britain."

Clement is convinced that even in the coronavirus pandemic, with people losing their jobs, there are great opportunities for people to become entrepreneurs.

"It's a good time for people to say I can't rely on a job. They'll sacrifice time with family to do a job. They'll work seven days a week to do overtime and almost sell their soul for their boss but the first opportunity a company gets to make people redundant they'll take it.

"When I worked for a merchant bank there were 250 people there. It was a good employer, but I don't think there are more than five people still working for that company from when I was there 20 years ago. They've either moved on or been made redundant.

"So, you can't put your trust in an employer to make you financially free and wealthy. You've got to take your own destiny into your own hands and make it work. You've got to take ownership."

He believes that every situation creates an opportunity, even in the rental market. "If people lose their jobs and can't afford their mortgages, they're going to be more likely to rent, so the rental market is going to be driven up. If they are single people, they are more likely to rent an HMO room in a shared house."

Clement buys all of his properties through auctions because he can complete the sale, refurbish the property and let it out in around three months – unlike a traditional house sale where there may be a chain which can break down and the deal is scuppered.

He watched one auction in the Midlands where around 200 properties were sold in one day during the Covid pandemic, he says, and many were sold at a fraction of the guide price.

Samuel bought his castle – Ribbesford House in Worcestershire – at auction. He agrees that the market during this period has been 'crazy' but adds a disclaimer that you should only buy at auction if you are properly trained, view the house that you are bidding on first and get surveys. Otherwise you can get burnt 'big time' at auction, he warns.

The number crunching is also crucial for Clement. "There isn't a column in my spreadsheet for emotions. I want to see the floor plan, find out what the transportation is like and what I can rent the rooms out for so that I can work out the return on investment. I will know roughly what the refurbishment costs will be."

Clement's experience of the Property Investors Crash Course was entirely positive. He credits the two-day event for giving him lots of information which helped him to scale up his business. But when he saw the negativity about Samuel Leeds on the internet, he admits he had doubts about him.

"Some of it was troubling and I thought maybe I didn't see that. It wasn't my experience and my opinion but if you listen to it enough, I suppose it can mess with your opinion."

Then there were reports in the media about Lord Sugar, the billionaire entrepreneur, denying giving Samuel business advice, which further fuelled his feeling of unease.

"I thought that's bad. I messaged Samuel on YouTube saying what happened there bro? It doesn't look good. But when I saw his rebuttal, I was like you know you're right."

Clement had become part of The Truth About Samuel Leeds Facebook group during this period but left when he received abuse at the hands of one commenter.

"I thought there was a lot of hatred and bitterness on there. I remember, one time, Samuel surprised his wife by taking her to Paris. I'm a pastor. Any man that takes care of his wife gets the thumbs up from me, so I posted that you've got to respect any man who takes care of his wife.

"I couldn't believe the negative response I got. I was like really? Are you being serious? It was wicked. One guy swore at me and told me to f*** off. The vitriol was so bad I left the group."

It was when he received a general email sent out from Property Investors, asking if he had ever benefited from Samuel's training, that he decided he needed to put the record straight.

"I had benefited, but for some reason because of the negativity I didn't really want to boast about it. So, I said I would talk about my own experiences. Why wouldn't I want to come on *Winners on a Wednesday* and celebrate that?

"Coming to Samuel's training was very helpful for me and I'm thankful for that. It was free and I implemented the information I got from it to scale up my business. It gave me confidence to do what I was thinking of doing and my passive monthly income has rocketed."

Some of the negativity surrounding Samuel Leeds has centred on claims that he pressure-sells his paid-for courses which Samuel has always denied as it is illegal. Clement says this was at odds with his own experience.

"I thoroughly enjoyed the crash course. I remember thinking this course must cost at least £20,000 to put on, so I was waiting for the big sell. It came late in the day when we were told about the paid-for training that you could sign up for, such as the *Deal Finding Extravaganza* but I was OK with that because the company has got to cover its costs. That's business."

He feels it is part of British culture to pull down successful people, but Samuel is doing a 'great job' and has helped a lot of other people too.

"It cost me a tank of diesel to get up to Birmingham and a night in hotel. His training was really helpful for me and it was a blessing."

Samuel is philosophical about the spotlight he has come under.

"Everything happens for a reason. I went through a challenging time. I had the press on me and there was a lot of negativity. I've grown through that. It's people like Clement who give me inspiration to keep going. He knows his market and his product, and he's got a massive heart to inspire others too. It's great to know I've been so influential in his success."

CLEMENT'S TIPS

"There's a lot of fear around property investing because if you get it wrong you can lose money, but that fear is mitigated by knowledge."

"Education and taking action are critical if you're going to make it in property. You also need energy, belief and persistence."

"Your environment makes an impact on you. If you surround yourself with property investors who are doing well, that's going to rub off on you."

Chapter 21 – Laurence LeFevre

100th Winner on a Wednesday who became financially free from one deal

It was a landmark moment when Laurence LeFevre became the 100th person to be interviewed by Samuel Leeds for his popular YouTube *Winners on a Wednesday* show.

 Laurence earned his place in Samuel's 'hall of fame' simply by implementing what his mentor taught him. His reward was to become financially free from just one deal after putting into practice what he learnt at the Property Investors Crash Course. He bought a block of flats by the seaside for a knockdown price and has never looked back since.

Having lost his job only the year before, it was a remarkable turnaround in his fortunes.

Laurence worked for ten years in sales recruitment until the long-established tour operator Thomas Cook collapsed in 2019 and he found himself out of work. Determined to take swift action, he went straight home and started searching on YouTube for strategies to replace his income.

That was when he came across Samuel's *Financial Freedom Challenge*. During the challenge Samuel proved that he could make enough money in a week from property investing to cover all his bills. The Property Investors' founder had no funds to start with when he set out to complete his goal.

"I thought this guy's done in one week what I've been trying to do for years, so I checked him out," recalls Laurence.

Then he booked himself on to the Property Investors Crash Course at the ExCeL convention centre in London in June 2019. He lapped up the free content which was given out.

"I probably learnt more in three hours at Samuel's course than I did in three years at university and having £30,000 of student debt."

He had been investing in stocks at that point for about eight years, but they were only giving him a return of three to five per cent. At the course Laurence discovered that if he put his money into property instead, he could achieve a return on investment of 20 to 25 per cent.

"I remember thinking if I just go home and sell all my stocks and put it into property, I can increase my cash flow five times and I'll be financially free within a year."

So, without delay, that is what he did.

"I took literally everything I learnt and just threw myself into it, rather than just carry on learning."

Laurence realised that he would need to obtain a mortgage in principle if he was to relaunch himself as a property entrepreneur. The only snag was that he no longer had a job. But then something Samuel had told his audience at the crash course came back to him.

"He said if you're going to buy a cash flow producing asset you don't need to have a full-time income yourself. It's based on the asset itself."

Even so, it was still an uphill struggle. At the start Laurence got 'laughed out of all the banks,' but eventually his persistence paid off and he obtained his mortgage promise – an agreement in principle from a lender to lend a certain amount before you have finalised the purchase of a property.

Samuel emphasises at his crash courses that if a house is a good investment, you will get lending. "Sometimes people say I can't get lending, but it's not about you. It's about the investments you can find. If you learn to find good deals everything else will follow."

Laurence found this to be true himself. "I spoke to ten different brokers. Half said no chance, you can't do this. Fast forward six months and they're emailing me asking who my lender is."

Having spent two months just talking to mortgage brokers, and eventually securing his mortgage promise, he then booked forty viewings in one week in Liverpool and Nottingham.

It was new territory to him on two fronts. He was unfamiliar with the cities, as he comes from south-east London, and he had never been on any viewings before. His research, however, told him that Liverpool was an up and coming place. He was also reassured by the fact that he had met many investors who had already bought properties in the city and done well.

Most of his due diligence was carried out on the ground. "I spoke to local estate agents and found out what they thought were the best postcodes. I talked to a lot of different taxi drivers as well and they warned me off certain roads. There was a house I was thinking of buying but when I spoke to a neighbour, they said there were a lot of gangs in the area."

Laurence also checked websites, such as SpareRoom and OpenRent, to find out if the rental demand was good in the areas he was targeting and what house prices were like.

"I just went through the crash course booklet and put all the information into a spreadsheet. I trusted the maths basically and made sure it worked."

Samuel says this type of due diligence is vital. "People ask me where the best investment areas are, but I can't give you a city because even in a place like Liverpool streets a quarter of a mile away from each other differ.

"Most people when they buy a property go with their gut feeling, for instance whether they like the area, but actually this is a process. You've got to check the right websites, speak to the right agents and ask the right questions."

Armed with the results of his research, Laurence finally settled on buying two houses. One of them cost £90,000. "I got it for £5,000 below the asking price but it was also £10,000 under what the owner had bought it for two years ago. That was because they were having a divorce, so technically I made £10,000 by just buying it."

He put down a deposit of £25,000 and now rents out the house for £590 a month to a surveyor and another tenant in receipt of housing benefit. His monthly mortgage payments amount to £150 and his profit is about £355.

Laurence calculates that his ROI on the two houses is 17 per cent, slightly below the minimum target of 20 per cent. It would have been higher, but there were unforeseen expenses, such as having to have a new boiler and a sensor.

Having a tenant who is on benefit is a good option, Samuel points out, because the rent is paid by the local authority and is therefore more or less guaranteed.

Sometimes in business you need courage and Laurence is not easily scared. At one time, he lived in the Amazon Jungle, and grew accustomed to being surrounded by creatures like giant anacondas and jaguars. He certainly proved he could hold his nerve with his next property deal in Blackpool.

His initial aim was to find a 'no money down,' rent-to-rent arrangement in the coastal resort. However, when he saw a block of ten flats for sale with a price tag of just £170,000, he realised it was too good an opportunity to miss.

"As soon as I saw it, I got my calculator out and my spreadsheet and went through everything we learnt on the crash course to work out what the cash flow and ROI would be. I thought this is unbelievable. If I can make this work, it will be making thousands and thousands of pounds every month."

Having been taught on the crash course to 'get comfortable with the uncomfortable,' he took the plunge and bid for it in an online auction. He admits he felt sick when the auctioneer announced he had made the highest offer.

"It was a nerve-wracking experience, especially when a week later the pandemic hit. I thought to myself, 'oh God what have I done,' but then I spoke with my management agency and they said everything about the property was just perfect. It worked really well, so I just had to trust the process, go with it and it's paying off."

Laurence used a bridging loan to purchase the apartments and now lets them out as furnished accommodation to visitors.

Two of the flats have yet to be renovated but the cash flow is already excellent, he says. "In August (2020), the revenue was £6,000 and that's in the middle of a pandemic. I can't believe a year's gone by and I'm making £6,000 to £7,000 a month. I'm still pinching myself now!"

Once life returns to normal, he plans to partner with local engineering firms and theatres, to ensure the block is fully booked.

Laurence found the flats through a deal sourcer who joined the Property Investors Academy and has also appeared on *Winners on a Wednesday*. He also found a rent-to-rent arrangement through her and she introduced him to a management agent who viewed the apartments with him. He has since taken on the agent.

"It's a small world when you get into property and everyone is so lovely as well. I always thought people in property would be too busy to help but they genuinely want to help. Anyone will meet you for a coffee pretty much."

Samuel agrees: "It's an industry where everybody wants everybody to win generally speaking. In my property world, the whole mantra is your success is our success. It's about helping people. So I'm really glad to hear that an academy member has helped Laurence out with what he's doing."

Laurence says he would never return to stocks as an investment. "Stocks is definitely the lazy way. It's hassle-free but you don't get the same income. You don't get capital growth and at the end of the day you're at the mercy of the stock market, whereas if I want to hold onto my house I don't have to sell. You have so much more control owning the property yourself and you can be so much more flexible with the financing on it."

His next step is to take on buy, refurbish and refinance projects and to keep expanding his property business.

"I want to see how big I can make it and I want a castle as well, like Samuel's one in Worcestershire. I want to try to get a bigger one though!"

Samuel describes Laurence's story as 'massively inspirational.'

"Laurence became financially free from buying a block of flats cheap as chips and is making so much more money than when he worked for someone else.

"I've now interviewed one hundred people for my *Winners on a Wednesday* show on YouTube. That's one hundred people who have had their finances revolutionised through property investing as a direct result of my training – and they're just the ones who shared their stories.

"I break down and simplify property investing, and train people how to live the life they deserve, so that, like Laurence, they don't have to rely on an employer any longer."

LAURENCE'S TIPS

"One of the biggest lessons I've learnt is if an opportunity is good, you'll always be able to find a lender."

"Make sure you trust in the numbers. Do your due diligence and take into account everything that could go wrong."

"If you want to invest in the housing market, just go to the Property Investors Crash Course. Ninety-nine per cent of the population don't know anything about investing for cash flow or passive income. You learn that straight away on the course. I'm making a lot more now than before when I was working for Thomas Cook."

Chapter 22 – Jamie Higgs

'Unstoppable' investor who gave up a well-paid job to get the life he wanted

When Jamie Higgs gave up his job to become a property entrepreneur, it came as a shock to his family and friends. He had a well-paid job and was on a good career path but felt that, ultimately, he could not achieve his dreams. Just over a year later Jamie is now reaping the rewards for having the courage of his own convictions after becoming financially independent with his first deal.

It was a Friday afternoon when Jamie was in his office, looking wistfully out of the window, wishing he could be somewhere else in that moment.

As he puts it, "The sun was blazing, and I was somewhere I didn't really want to be in the sense there were other things I wanted to do.

"I didn't want to miss any of my sons' sport. I wanted to be free to watch both of them enjoy their sport. I just thought there's got to be more to life."

Jamie had worked his way up the ladder to become a leader in logistics after starting out in a warehouse job at 18.

"I did enjoy it. I'd worked hard and never had a day off, but I wanted to get out of the rat race because I was living someone else's dream. I was setting goals for myself, but I was on a train that was never going to get me to that destination. I was always going to fall short."

Then fate intervened. In December 2018, the tolls on the two bridges over the River Severn, which connect England to Wales, were removed. As a result, the value of his house in Newport in South Wales shot up and he pulled out some equity.

Having decided he wanted to become a property investor, Jamie spent a few months devouring Samuel Leeds' videos on YouTube. Then, in May 2019, he attended the Property Investors Crash Course with his wife.

The importance of training was always paramount in his mind. "I wanted to invest but I didn't know how to invest in property. I didn't know all the different strategies. In my work, it was always you train, you educate and then you move forward rather than just dive in.

"I'd looked at a few other trainers. All I had from them was a call saying pay me some money and I'll send you some videos. That's not what I was looking for. When we went to the crash course that was it for me. I was in. There was real high energy in the room."

Jamie put the money which he had released from his home into joining the Property Investors Academy.

In July, he quit his job and took advantage of some gardening leave to become compliant as a deal sourcer. He also attended the academy's *Rent-to-Rent* course and networked 'like crazy' in his local area to find mentors.

"I'm not saying it's right for everyone. It was a calculated risk, but it was right for me at the time. I had some funds in the background and I was prepared for it. I've always had a good job. With the career path I was on, to say 'no, I'm going this way' was a bit of a shock to everyone but I've had nothing but support from friends and family including my 'super supportive' wife.

"I knew I probably had about 12 months to get everything going and start to get some income."

With the need to gain a quick cash flow, Jamie initially focused his efforts on looking for properties to package and sell. He co-sourced one deal with another Property Investors Academy member, earning himself a fee of £3,000. However, after going on the academy's *Pull Out All Your Money* course, Jamie realised that the buy, refurbish and refinance strategy might be more lucrative.

"I remember saying to Samuel if this works and I can get out of the rat race, I'll be forever in his debt and I'll be doing a *Winners on a Wednesday* video. Now I've done exactly that!"

After the Property Investors Crash Course, Jamie met up with a friend in his local area who was already a successful property investor. Jamie told him his budget and said that he was looking for properties which he could renovate to increase their value.

He was at the academy's *Rent-to-Rent* course on a Friday when his friend rang him.

"He was saying, Jamie I think I've got a deal for you in Newport. It doesn't fit my strategy. It's a commercial/residential property which is very tired and needs work. The only issue is the landlord is in Spain."

The distance was no problem for Jamie. By the next day he was on a flight to Spain to negotiate the deal. "I wanted to speak to the landlord face to face. I thought by doing that, we could come to a deal. Everything I'd learnt about on the *Pull All Your Money Out* course and also the knowledge I had from the academy about buy, refurbish and refinance projects was sinking in."

It turned out the landlord was from the same area and they had acquaintances in common. Jamie was also helped by being aware of local house prices.

The property consisted of two shops with flats above and even though it needed work, Jamie was confident he could add value.

Having made an offer while he was out there, they agreed a price of £275,000 and in December 2019 the renovation work began.

Friends and family helped out. All the materials for the refurbishment were provided on an account with a friend so that Jamie didn't have to pay for them until the refinancing stage.

"Everyone knew I was 100 per cent committed to the project. On Christmas Eve we were in there painting the shop."

In total, he put in £85,000 of his own money and took out a bridging loan of £230,000, while the renovation cost £27,000.

Once the work was finished in September 2020, Jamie was careful to get the timing of the revaluation right. At the time there was still uncertainty over Britain's withdrawal from the European Union. He had been advised the valuer might 'keep a bit back' if Brexit was still up in the air, so he arranged the valuation after the UK's departure from the EU in January 2020.

It proved to be a wise step. The valuation came out at £425,000 and he then refinanced the property. The returns have been impressive.

"We got 70 per cent of £425,000 and pulled out £297,500. We left £15,000 in the deal. It grosses £42,000 a year in rents and the net profit is about £24,000."

The previous landlord was earning just £105 per week for the whole block by comparison.

Jamie admits it was 'scary' having a bridging loan during the coronavirus pandemic but rolled up the interest to defer the repayment. "Interest on a bridging loan is quite high but it's a very useful tool to get you what you want."

In hindsight, he would have done things slightly differently. "Because I was deemed a non-experienced landlord the rates were a bit higher. I would never say no to the deal again but if I did it again, I would get some landlord experience beneath my belt with a small single buy-to-let and then you can get bigger and bigger."

The fact that it was a commercial purchase enabled him to split the titles on completion and add gardens which proved to be an attraction during the lockdown.

"There are three one-bedroom flats and each one has got its own private garden. Having an outside space during that time was really good. I had 50 to 60 enquiries per unit and they all rented out within 24 hours.

"The two commercial units were rented within 48 hours. It was an amazing deal."

When Jamie made the transition from being employed to running his own property business, he used his leave to learn about tax, cash flow and setting up a limited company.

Now he is a full-time property investor but is still educating himself all the time to further his knowledge of investing in the housing market. He has private mentors and spends a few hours each day with a specialist mortgage broker to pick up tips from deals coming in. He also attends as many property events as possible, networks, makes Zoom calls and supports his wife in her business.

His 17-year-old son has been learning about property too. He joined his father's business when he left school which coincided with Jamie setting out on a new career path.

"We've all read *Rich Dad Poor Dad* and you get that eureka moment where you think I've been doing this wrong. I said to my son you don't have to get a job or go to uni. You can come on this journey with me and we can learn together. He gets financial reward for it as part of the limited company.

"He's a good boy and switched on. I want him to have the freedom to follow his dream. I'll offer my 13-year-old son the same opportunity as well. I want to allow my children and their children to do what they want to do, rather than go into the rat race."

Leaving a legacy for his family is Jamie's principal reason for going into property, but he also wants to be able to help his mother-in-law who is unwell.

Jamie's latest project is refurbishing two flats in Llanelli which he bought for £50,000. Estate agents estimate they will fetch between £145,000 to £185,000 once the work is complete. He expects to sell them for £160,000.

"The renovation will cost around £40,000 and I should be able to pull all my money out. The bigger the problem, the more negotiating you can do and the more value you can add."

The *Buy, Refurbish and Refinance Masterclass* course at the Property Investors Academy has given him the knowledge and confidence which comes with that to pull off such a deal.

Jamie says he is lucky to be in the right area. Capital appreciation and rents are good, and many other investors, including fellow academy members, are doing well in South Wales. Houses can still be picked up for as little as £50,000 and he will be looking for more commercial/residential opportunities along the M4 corridor and elsewhere.

"I believe there's going to be lot of commercial property coming up soon, whether that's locally or along the M4 corridor. I'm not fazed by the numbers as such. You put an equal amount of effort in. If the deal stacks, the deal will stack.

"Commercial purchases come with a few benefits. You don't pay any stamp duty on the first £150,000 of the agreed sale price. On my first deal in Newport I paid £2,200 stamp duty.

"There is a lot of doom and gloom at the moment but there are some fantastic opportunities coming up within the property world."

Samuel Leeds agrees: "There's a saying: wherever there's doom and gloom observe the masses and do the opposite. I know everyone's worried and scared but that's when you should be getting in."

Jamie describes the support from the Property Investors Academy as 'great.' He receives a monthly business call with a mentor in a Mastermind group of five and still has some courses to do.

He also used a book on deal sourcing by Alasdair Cunningham, a senior member of the company's management team, as a template to set himself up for selling deals to investors. The deal which Jamie packaged up and co-sourced was in South Wales.

The property was on sale for £50,000 with a projected end value of £90,000 to £95,000 after renovation.

"The refurbishment cost was about £15,000 and the legal fees £2,500, bringing the total to £67,500. If you achieve a valuation of £90-£95,000 when you refinance at 75 per cent loan to value, you're probably going to pull all your money out, depending on what your end value is. 0.75 times the end value gives you the money you're going to pull out.

"The investor was happy with the deal. I had viewed nine other properties that day when I saw the for sale sign on this property lying on the floor. The estate agent said someone had pulled out when I questioned it. It was lucky I suppose.

"I'm not expecting to be a millionaire in a few years, I'm just on a steady road, building slowly with new projects and using funds all the way through to continue to invest. The challenge for me will be when I start investing outside of my patch."

Samuel praises Jamie. "When you put yourself in the right place at the right time, with the right knowledge, you're just going to get lucky. And he joined the academy and opened himself up and said I'm looking for deals."

Jamie describes his journey so far in property as a rollercoaster. "You get your highs off the back of an event and you're flying and then nothing's happening and then you go back up again. When you're in the middle of a deal, you've got all these issues popping up like dealing with solicitors and planning permission and riding these waves but ultimately with consistent action you're going to get there.

Samuel agrees that It is a process. "If you follow the steps you will get there."

He is highly impressed with his student's progress so far: "The reason Jamie has done so well is because he understood the importance of gaining property knowledge and put aside money from refinancing his house to invest in training.

"He pulled off a corker of a deal with his first investment. It not only made him financially free but gave him over £100,000 of equity which is incredible.

"To achieve that deal he flew to Spain to negotiate with the landlord. That's the kind of thing which separates successful and unsuccessful people. He's put in lots of hours to get where he is. He's unstoppable."

JAMIE'S TIPS

"If you want to become a property investor but don't know where to start, look at Samuel Leeds' YouTube videos. It's free content."

"Educate yourself as much as you can. Don't just dive in. Make sure you understand your strategy."

"Look at Samuel's YouTube videos first and then go to the Property Investors Crash Course. If you go for it, go for it and choose your strategy."

"Look for someone who's just ahead of you as an investor. You don't have to reinvent the wheel. You just do exactly what they do."

Chapter 23 – Adam Flynn

22-year-old changes his and his family's life on the back of attending the Property Investors Crash Course

Propelled by the desire to change his life, Adam Flynn attended the Property Investors Crash Course at the age of only 21 to learn how to make money in the housing market. Now he is a full-time deal sourcer at the helm of a unique family property business attracting investors from far and wide.

Success has come quickly. In just two months alone, Adam and his fellow directors, including his brother, father and uncle, have banked around £30,000 from deals and are going from strength to strength all the time.

It was Adam's twin brother who drew his attention to Property Investors' founder Samuel Leeds and his YouTube videos. They watched them together and then enrolled on the crash course to find out more.

Adam had no previous experience of property other than when he was younger and his dad, who is a builder by trade, taught him how to fit kitchens and bathrooms. So, the course was a real eye-opener to him because it showed him how, with a little capital, he could derive an income from finding houses for investors.

At the time, Adam had been working for three years as an insolvency administrator but was looking for a way out.

"I've always wanted to do something more than the nine to five. I've always been quite entrepreneurial," he explains.

In January 2020, the family property company was incorporated, and two months later Adam became a compliant sourcer. This means he has fulfilled all the legal requirements which permit him to charge investors for finding property deals.

Having completed the formalities, Adam was raring to go, but two months later the UK government imposed a lockdown to stop the spread of the coronavirus. Rather than put the business on hold, Adam and his fellow directors made sure they used their time profitably. His friend was also on board by now and they started making preparations so that when life got back to normal again, they would be ready.

"We were all working from home and had time to build the brand, get a logo and get our social media up and running. We got everything else sorted, so that when we could go to an investors' group, we would look professional but then be open and transparent and say, look we're new to the game.

"This is our business model and thankfully we've been in touch with investors who've given us a chance because we are so open with them. They like the idea of what we're doing."

Their business proposition was to offer a complete hands-off service to busy professionals looking to put their savings into an investment property in the north of England.

Adam's role was to find the deals and negotiate the purchase price, while his father and uncle, who is also a builder, would refurbish the properties and manage the projects.

What made their model different was that they would be teaming up with social housing providers in need of rental accommodation. All the conveyancing would be done by the company and the housing association or council would provide the tenants.

Before they could turn this vision into a reality, however, they had to find buyers for their deals. The tactic, which they used, was simple. Adam and his brother and friend contacted anyone who looked like they had a good job on LinkedIn.

"We messaged everyone under the sun who we thought could be wealthy and asked them if they would be interested in investing in property," recalls Adam.

Out of 50 messages they hoped to get at least one lead. Through sheer persistence they found their first investor – the owner of a dental practice in London who wanted to invest in property in the north. Three of his offers had been accepted before the Covid-19 crisis but had then fallen through.

"He was coming up north and doing it all himself until he found us. He hadn't heard of the social housing idea. We sold him on it, so he thought he would give us a go."

The investor was keen to buy a property in the centre of Manchester. However, prices had gone up ridiculously and the market was highly competitive, says Adam. So, he cast his net wider and secured a deal on a buy-to-let on The Wirral, near Liverpool.

Since then he has sourced and sold a total of eight deals. Four were buy-to-lets and four HMOs, including three four-bedroom houses and a six-bed property. Their fee for sourcing and packaging a buy-to-let is £2,500 plus VAT and £4,000 plus VAT for an HMO. They also charge a project management fee. This is worked out at 10 per cent of the refurbishment cost, with a minimum charge of £1,000. So, if the cost of the renovation is £30,000, the project management fee is £3,000 plus VAT.

"You're paying for a service," Adam emphasises. "It's hands free. The investors don't have to get involved. The money goes directly into their bank account and we sort everything out. They don't have to come up north. They don't even have to see the property."

There are many advantages of working with social housing organisations, he adds. They offer the investor a guaranteed rental income with no voids because the rates are very competitive. They also provide tenant damage cover and pay the utility bills – and there are no management fees, all of which minimises the risks involved. As well as that, the returns are far better than the bank's rate of interest which has hit an all-time low in recent months.

"The capital needed to buy an investment property in the north of England is approximately £25,000. We typically achieve net yields of eight per cent plus. If you purchase with a mortgage, you can expect to achieve a return on investment of at least 15 per cent."

His father and uncle each has a 20 per cent share in the business as an incentive to complete jobs quickly and efficiently.

It is an approach which allows Adam to concentrate on the sourcing. "Hopefully we can get the processes in place to do ten houses a month. They'll be able to cope with that and we're all making money as a family."

Adam left his employment at the end of August 2020 and the offer on that all-important first deal was accepted on September 9. Since then the investors have come flooding in.

"We barely go out and find investors now. They come to us through posting on social media and us showing them what we're doing, and we get referrals as well.

"I had one telephone call with a barrister in London who afterwards voice noted all her barrister friends in the office and they've now all got in touch wanting to buy from us.

"I don't know if she was impressed with me or the concept, or the business model but after one conversation, without even buying from us, she is already recommending us."

Adam prefers to find the investor before the deal. "A lot of people say the deal comes first but in my opinion it's the other way around. Why would you go looking for something and not have someone to buy it? You need to know what the investor wants."

Samuel Leeds agrees. "All you are going to do is find the deal and you're not going to be able to sell it, and then you're going to upset the estate agent."

Bad deal sourcers can hamper the prospects of the good ones whose reputation hangs on being able to find someone to buy a property once they have agreed a price on it.

Adam has already found some Manchester agents are reluctant to do business with people working in his sector because of offers often falling through at a late stage.

"Around the city centre sometimes they won't take a viewing off a deal sourcer now, or they want proof of funds from the start. This is no problem to us because when we sign an investor up, before we start looking, we get them to sign a contract. We also ask them to show us proof of funds and ID to comply with money laundering regulations. Everything is up front so that we know they're serious and not messing around.

"We get the investor involved before we put the offer in, so we know he's buying that deal. We've never had an estate agent annoyed with us because we've pulled out. We've always gone through with everything we've done. Now we're getting a name for ourselves in certain areas and getting properties offered to us. They know we are cash buyers because we do a lot of HMOs from the social housing leads."

Samuel believes it is vital to be reliable. "I think it's so important you don't sabotage your relationship with estate agents because they are key. And you want them passing you off market deals."

He is impressed that Adam has managed to attract investors at such a young age. "It's so inspiring when he's still only 22. I get men in their fifties complaining to me that they can't find any investors."

Adam's response to this is that you have to have the right mindset. Coming from a business background has also helped him, he admits.

"I've worked in the corporate world. I've got an idea of finance. For a living I worked with businesses that didn't do well. They were going into liquidation and administration, so I know exactly what not to do and I've learnt from their mistakes."

Despite this, he is adamant that without the Property Investors Crash Course he wouldn't be where he is now. "I know Samuel has had a lot of stick from the BBC and stuff but I'm just a normal lad from Bury in Manchester and I can honestly say without coming to that crash course I wouldn't be in property. I would just be in my job still on a modest wage."

Adam has a strong work ethic and has never been one to put his feet up after work and watch television. When he was employed, he was always networking to win business for his company and is still doing so these days, even though he has left.

"All these investors we're getting now, if they need tax advice, mortgage brokers or accountants, I refer them to my old firm because they provide all of those services. I've passed on so much work to them. They're loving it."

As a consequence, the partners in the firm have shown an interest in investing with Adam's property business.

His day-to-day life has changed considerably too since coming to the crash course. "I'll wake up and I might not necessarily know what I'm going to do that day. I might do some admin, or I'll get a call to view a house or have a few calls with investors. You might have weekends where you have to work, so if you do get a bit of free time in the week you don't feel guilty about going to the gym or doing something you want to do – because you've always got to be switched on."

He prides himself on being there for his investors when they need him. "They text me and get a response straight away unless I'm doing something in that moment or driving."

His dedication has produced handsome rewards already. "With the sourcing company, we've made about £20,000 in two months and £10,000 in project management fees."

Adam stresses that for anyone who might think that being a property entrepreneur is an easy ride, it is not. "I will be working hard for that project management fee because I've got to bring in contractors in different areas, but I'm proud of what I've achieved so far."

His father and uncle have the option of putting down their tools in two to three years and concentrating on project management full-time if they can grow the business. This would help them 'massively.'

"My dad was on a zero-hours contract and needed to be employed to sort his mortgage situation, which we've helped him with, but ideally they want to be off the tools."

The next step, though, is to bring his brother and his 'mate' into the business full time. The younger directors may also settle for a passive income in a few years' time. For the moment, however, they remain eager for more success.

Adam takes £2,000 net a month out of the business, but all dividends get put into a holding company, which the family has also set up to invest in property themselves.

"We don't want a passive income as yet because we're young, but we'll make that pot as big as we can by flipping, flipping, flipping. Maybe when we're 30, and we've got £1m, we'll invest that at 20 per cent. That's a £200,000 passive income for us. We might have that option to never have to work again in our life which I think is what anyone would like.

"But at the moment we're hungry. Why would we want to sit back now? We may as well work hard while we're hungry because it's exciting."

Adam says his reason for going into property was initially because he was money-obsessed, but now that has changed.

"My why now is to have a good life to have options and freedom."

Samuel is impressed by what Adam has achieved within just a year of coming to the Property Investors Crash Course in Birmingham, in October 2019. "Adam has really created a unique proposition to investors. I think that's why he's winning. Yes, I teach people the process, but he's taken that and adapted it and made it his own. I really commend him for doing that.

"He could have said I'm 21. I've never done this before, and I've got no track record. But instead he said I've had experience of business in my job and I'm going to flip that into a positive. He focused on what he did have. Then he found investors and delivered well. Now he's getting lots of referrals and people wanting to buy from him. It's so inspiring."

ADAM'S TIPS

"Go to the Property Investors Crash Course to get an idea of all the strategies."

"Don't do all the strategies at once. Concentrate on one of them at first."

"Find someone who's doing what you're doing and just ask them if you can have an hour's call with them to see what their processes are. You might be able to help them too."

"One thing I would say to my old self is don't just leave work if you've got no company, no compliance or investors. In my last month in work, I had investors pestering me for deals. I'd say give me a month before I'm full time. So, you need to be at that stage before you even think about leaving work in my opinion."

"With your first investor you might have to take a reduction in your fees, otherwise if you go charging £5,000 a deal at the start you're never going to get anywhere. You may need to do this on the first couple of deals to get a track record that you can post on social media. Obviously, make sure the investor is serious first though."

Chapter 24 – Jay Udeh

'I wouldn't have these HMO leads without Leeds' – poet pens a special tribute to Samuel

Students of Samuel Leeds who go on to become full-time property entrepreneurs are happy to show their appreciation by sharing their experiences and tips on *Winners on a Wednesday*. Property poet Jay Udeh went one step further by writing a rhythmic tribute dedicated to Samuel which he read out to his mentor while being interviewed for his YouTube series. It was Jay's way of saying a special thank you for helping him become a successful deal sourcer at a crisis point in his life.

The former economics teacher's pathway into business began with the Property Investors Crash Course in December 2019. He was so incentivised by Samuel's mantra of 'big energy means big bank,' that within a month of attending the event, he had sourced an HMO deal in Stoke-on-Trent.

His plan was to pass the deal to a co-sourcer who would sell it to an investor, and they would share the finder's fee. Unfortunately for Jay, his promising start was derailed by the coronavirus pandemic. All conveyancing ground to an abrupt halt as house moves were delayed by the UK government to slow the spread of the disease.

With no funds coming through from the transaction, Jay, who had recently got married and had a baby, decided to go back into teaching, having done this for the past ten years. But then he was hit with another blow when the offer of a job fell through at the last minute, leaving him in the lockdown of March 2020 with no money coming in.

It was disheartening, Jay, admits, although he recognised there was a choice to be made after reading Napoleon Hill's best-selling self-help book, *Think and Grow Rich*.

"*Think and Grow Rich* talks about success consciousness. So, you can have a situation [like mine] and let that stop you or you can say, I'm going to apply for five or six other jobs – or let me just stay in property for a bit longer."

Having already gained confidence from sourcing a deal, he decided to 'stay in the field' and keep pushing himself to make a go of being a property entrepreneur. It was clear to Jay that he would need to invest in education to improve his prospects and so he paid £1,000 for further training with Property Investors. In the circumstances, it was a brave step, but Jay maintained his faith in himself that he could succeed.

"Although I didn't get one single penny for six months, that deal kept me going. I knew if I spent a month with Samuel on training, it would push me forward," he says.

Jay signed up for Property Investors' *Lease Options Boot Camp* so that he could sell lease option deals to investors and then joined the advanced coaching programme.

"I thought of the advanced coaching as my lockdown training. What was great is that we got the content up front, with calls once a week from Samuel and four weekly webinars on a Monday night which was a great way to start the week.

"I think the key was to take massive action in between the calls to get the most out of it. If you get information that's one thing, but no one learns to ride a bike from just reading about it. You've got to go out and do it."

Jay was determined to be proactive. He completed a 14-day lease options challenge as part of his training and then began 'prospecting.' The Gumtree classified ads website provided him with lots of names of agents and landlords to ring.

"I didn't secure a lease option deal, but I became very comfortable with the whole process of calling people and looking for deals," Jay recalls.

After this, he decided to look instead for rent-to-rent agreements which, in his opinion, were less complicated to negotiate than lease options. This time he jumped onto the SpareRoom site to find leads. On his fifth call, he spoke to the owner of a five-bedroom house in Coventry who was advertising it for rent.

Jay explained that he could offer the landlord a fixed amount each month if they were willing to allow someone else to let the rooms out at a higher rate and keep the profit.

"The landlord lived in London and during Covid times wasn't bothered to come up and down to check the property, so we agreed a guaranteed monthly rent of £1,250 which would make the investor a profit of £700 a month."

Jay passed the deal to a co-sourcer who sold it to an investor on his database. It was a win-win situation for everyone concerned, he points out. "I love the fact property is about inter-dependence. It solved the landlord's problem and the investor was happy too." And, of course, Jay and his fellow sourcer received a fee for facilitating the arrangement.

"If someone can make £1,500 and I can make £1,500 for a deal, we're going to both work hard to get that deal over the line, rather than it being only an 'I win' scenario. When both parties are winning, we share the energy and the experience. We share the joy and some of the pain as well, so I think shared experience is much more powerful than just relying on doing it by yourself."

Samuel agrees: "There's a saying, if you want to go fast, go alone. If you want to go far, go together. If you look at people who are winning in property, they are the ones who say I'm in this for the long game. Invest in myself. I'm going to network, collaborate and give value to the community because what goes around comes around. It's the difference between farming and hunting. A farmer will plant seeds and wait for growth. A hunter wants a quick deal and has to go hunting every time they go hungry."

Environment is everything, he adds. "Who you hang around with is who you become."

Jay's investment in property training has more than paid off. In the space of three months, he has sourced a total of seven property deals, selling them through a co-sourcer and picking up £8,000 in commission.

In time, he hopes to take on some of the properties he finds himself, but says he is 'unequivocally focused' on becoming a 'deal sourcing machine' first.

Mindset has been fundamental in his progress. A strong desire to succeed, as well as hard work have helped put Jay on the road to making money from the housing market. He sent out 250 letters to landlords in Coventry to try to get more property deals. In each letter, he enclosed a sachet of tea to attract their attention.

Out of those letters, he now has access to two portfolios and three other properties which he intends to sell as rent-to-rent deals to social housing providers.

"These organisations need accommodation in bulk for homeless people. There's a big demand for that. So, I'm hoping I can match these portfolios with social housing providers, rather than looking for individual investors."

Jay will charge a commission per property to reflect the time and money he has spent acquiring the knowledge and skills to find and negotiate deals which investors will want.

"Before the Property Investors Crash Course, I didn't know how to work out the return on investment or what landlord letters were. I didn't know how to find a portfolio. I've had to invest into this, so I've got to value my skills by charging a middle fee. I will still be co-sourcing but ultimately there will be bigger projects as well that I will be dealing with."

Samuel says this is a really smart move as housing associations will pay the fee if they want the accommodation.

Jay had previously tried his hand at Forex trading and network marketing to increase his income but had dismissed property investing as being too complicated and boring.

His experience at the Property Investors Crash Course taught him otherwise when he was invited to come on stage and pitch a deal to around 1,000 people. He also had to make calls and found himself immersed in the world of running a property business.

"I'm a teacher and I was so impressed by the crash course. There was group work, good interaction and people were going upstairs to do their calls. They were moving around rather than just being like zombies. You need high energy to retain what you're being taught.

"But with any training twenty per cent is Samuel Leeds, eighty per cent me. Ultimately, he can't do my press-ups or pick up the phone for me."

Samuel endorses this view wholeheartedly. "What I can do is give people the process, all the steps they need to take to become a property investor and encourage them. If you follow that process, success is going to be inevitable. Knowledge is important, but you've got to believe it's possible and say I'm a winner, I'm going to go out and get some deals in the next few months.

"One of the reasons Jay has been successful is because he has taken mad action. There are a lot of talkers out there, but there are very few who will walk the walk. I'm really proud of him and I really appreciate that he's written a poem for me. No one's ever done that for me before! I'm really touched by it and thankful.

"Every week I interview one of my success students for the Winners on a Wednesday series on my YouTube channel and it's things like this that give me my mission."

JAY'S TIPS

"If you want to be a property entrepreneur, know why you want it and write it down. I wanted to become successful for my wife and son. Now I'm spending more time at home which is nice."

"Once you know why you want it, consider how much you want to make each month. Have a target."

"Then decide how you are going to achieve that income and get the cash flowing. GPS always gives you multiple routes, but you've got to choose the one that will be the most efficient and the fastest – and also that will avoid some of the traffic and speed bumps you are going to encounter in any entrepreneur's journey. It's definitely about taking the right route at the right time and then bigger things come along."

"Of course, you can get educated on YouTube or take a course, but it has to be cemented with a deep desire to succeed. If you really want to do it, you won't give up when it's difficult."

Extract from Jay's ode to Samuel

Until October 2019 before Covid I avoided property

Saw your YouTube videos at a social media distance

Until your crash course broke the resistance

Crash course changed course

People learning

Strong force

Property fun as Sam talks

First time and I present a deal on stage

First time and I saw everybody engaged

First time and I worked out ROI on a deal

First time and property became real

Transformation not just information

Phone calls, calculations, collaboration, dedications

For free

What a foundation

I wouldn't have these HMO leads without Leeds

Now rent-to-rent pays the rent

Wife content because of your content

Always giving out your resources as soon as

Giving out money like Rishi Sunak

Haters really jab you

Upper cut you each day

But you get off the canvas

Fight back like AJ

Chapter 25 – Chris Jaap

Ex-RAF engineer is flying high, sourcing investment properties for wealthy clients in London and Dubai

Chris Jaap is one of Property Investors' most successful students, having appeared twice on Winners on a Wednesday to share his experience and advice. His portfolio includes 20 rent-to-rent deals in the North West. He also runs a successful deal sourcing business, working amongst others with wealthy investors in London and Dubai.

There have been challenges particularly during 2020. Due to the coronavirus pandemic, he lost around £10,000 worth of bookings for his serviced accommodation early on in the crisis. However, Chris has picked himself up by adapting his business to changing market conditions.

When the father-of-one first appeared on Samuel Leeds' popular YouTube Winners on a Wednesday series, he had recently gone into property full-time and sealed two rent-to-rent deals.

Since then he has gone from strength to strength, expanding his rent-to-rent interests tenfold in the space of just 18 months.

Chris was previously a busy contractor who installed communications systems in air traffic control towers. His job meant he was hardly ever at home. He travelled throughout the country and also abroad before that with the Royal Air Force as an electronics engineer.

It was an interesting and varied career. He provided mission critical support for the Eurofighter Typhoon combat aircraft in UK defence operations across Europe, Asia and the Middle East. He also built secure communications networks for use by military personnel on active duty in rugged terrain, as well as maintaining navigational aids and surveillance equipment.

His hobby took him all over the world as well. He represented Wales in ten-pin bowling and was the RAF's top player. But when he got married and had a son Charlie in 2017, his priorities changed. He decided he wanted a more settled lifestyle and looked to property as a way of helping him to achieve that.

One benefit of being constantly on the road was that Chris had time while he was staying in hotels to read up about investing in the housing market. There was plenty of information available to help him in his research – including the huge amount of free content Property Investors' founder Samuel Leeds shares on his YouTube channel.

Chris drank it all in. He watched Samuel's videos and read his books, listened to podcasts and then booked himself on the Property Investors Crash Course. After attending the two-day event, he signed up for the company's *Deal Finding Extravaganza* course.

"I thought this is it for me. I knew I was the sort of person who would keep going to make something successful," he recalls.

So, he gave up his work to join the Property Investors Academy, where he found a network of like-minded people who could support each other on their journey to becoming entrepreneurs.

As Samuel stresses: "When you join the academy, you're not just paying for information and implementation. You're paying for the environment and network of friends it gives you. For me that's vitally important."

Chris agrees: "That was my biggest reason for doing it and that is the biggest thing I've taken from it. The network is everything for me."

It was a leap of faith quitting his job, he says, but he felt that if his sole focus was on property, he could make a go of it with the help of the academy's comprehensive training modules.

His confidence in his own ability and the training paid off. After a year Chris had secured rent-to-rent deals on six HMO properties in Chester and two in Deeside – with between five and nine bedrooms each – in addition to eight, furnished en suite rooms in Liverpool, which were let to short stay visitors.

In each case, Chris negotiated a rent-to-rent agreement with the owner. As part of the deal he pays the landlord a guaranteed monthly rent for the accommodation and then lets it out at a profit.

In return, he agreed to take over all the management and maintenance of the property, including finding and vetting tenants, collecting rents and dealing with any problems. He also gave the rooms a fresh lick of paint, had new carpets fitted and brought in furniture to create a high-end look.

Three of the properties alone were making a monthly profit of £2,500, while five others were earning him around £3,600 a month. With the studio apartments in Liverpool also generating thousands of pounds a month, Chris became financially independent.

"I systemised the business once I got to the point where I'd got more than 10 properties," Chris explains.

Having a property and lettings manager freed his time to set up a sourcing company which increased his knowledge and experience of the market substantially.

Reaching that point where he was able to systemise his business came a lot quicker than he anticipated. However, like many other investors, Chris and his business partner, Patrick Welsh, who he met on the academy, have been badly hit by the Covid-19 outbreak.

"Our studio apartments in the city centre were generating £2,000-£3,000 in a good month just from weekend bookings. We picked up a lot of custom from football traffic and stag do's.

"Covid wiped it completely. It cancelled every booking we had and that was back in February. We had bookings worth £8,000 to £10,000 gross up until September. We knew back then we had that ready. Then it was gone. It hurt in the chest."

With Airbnb limiting UK bookings to key workers and essential visits during the lockdown, they realised they had to act quickly to replace the lost income.

"When you're doing a rent-to-rent, an empty bed is profit loss, so you need to be on top of your game. We've changed the clientele to contractors now, but we really had to push to get them through marketing campaigns, Facebook and Instagram ads – everything we could think of to do. We even went as far as visiting some of the sites in the local area where contractors were working, just to promote the business and show them what we could offer."

They also reduced their charges in response to the new situation. "Liverpool has quite a lot on offer in terms of serviced accommodation, so we've had to look at bringing the prices down to reflect this. It's been a difficult time."

Despite these difficulties, they have added four flats to their rent-to-rent portfolio – bringing the total to 20 properties owned by 13 separate landlords.

Chris credits his support network in the Property Investors Academy for helping him to negotiate a better deal with the owner of the flats.

"The landlord wanted quite a large amount for the block because he knows they're nice flats. He also knows the area and what rent he could get. It was members on the academy who suggested I lower the price but offer to do the furnishings. You can always offset the furnishings on finance or lease them.

"I had to pay a little more upfront, but that allowed me to have a lower rent for a longer period. Now we're taking about £1,500 a month on this one deal alone."

The whole deal, he says, came about due to a set of fortuitous circumstances.

"I get on well with the carpet fitter who fitted the carpets for me for one of my first jobs and has done other work for me. He was passing by whilst this place was getting refurbished by the vendor and just walked in to see if he could sell carpets to them. He ended up passing my details to the landlord and we negotiated the deal.

"Since then we've created a good friendship with this vendor who has asked me to look at another property in the city centre. We've not been able to agree on anything just yet but again you don't know where these leads are going to come from."

Chris' sourcing company, Nordic Property Solutions, is also flourishing, bringing in finder's fees of £3,000-£5,000 on several deals.

"We send out deals quite regularly," he says. "Recently we had a fantastic deal which we've packaged and are project managing for one of our investors. That's going to be an almost all money out deal and cash flowing over £1,000 net a month, so they're happy.

"We charge a separate project management fee if the client wants it. Some of the investors we work with are based in Dubai and London. One investor says he wants to build up a portfolio aggressively. So, it's people who want to move fast. We've got the criteria for these guys and we're ready to move."

When asked what he believes comes first – the deal or the investor – he replies: "It's the one question I was constantly asking myself and everybody. Now that I'm on the other side of the fence people are asking me. Personally, I like to find the investor to find the deal for them so then you know what you're looking for and you can say I found this. It's exactly what you want.

"Then you can promote that – look what we found for this investor. This is what we can offer. However, if you're good at finding deals but don't have an investor you can co-source with somebody and then you can get recognised for your ability to find the deal."

With each investment property he handles, Chris can feel himself growing in experience: "Every deal that you don't necessarily get over the line, you learn something from it, and you bring it to the next one."

Chris describes his journey in property as a rollercoaster with massive ups and downs, one of those being the pandemic but he also reached a breaking point.

"I am a very strong-minded person. I was in the military for 13 years before I came into property investing. I'm quite confident in my abilities and myself as an individual, but there was a time last year when I had some problems.

"I'd just taken on three or four deals at the same time and it overwhelmed me because I didn't know how I was going to pay for them or get the refurbishments done. I broke down but relying on the people around you and the friends you make, that pulled me back into normality.

"Finding solutions to the problems I had back then allowed me to progress as a business. You can think, I just can't do this. It's not going to happen, I'm ruined, but if you just stop and think, what's the solution, find that, then that helps you. The experience made me grow as a person so that I could be a bit calmer."

Since becoming a property entrepreneur, Chris's life has changed immeasurably. He is in control of where and when he works.

"I travelled a lot with all my jobs. I was always away, abroad for ten days at a time with two days off. I thought enough was enough. When you get married and have a kid you want to come home and be with your family. That was my reason for going into property."

Before his second Winners on a Wednesday appearance Chris told Samuel that he had another pressing appointment back home – to carve some pumpkins with the family!

Samuel approves: "That's really important. You can spend your whole life working crazy hours to make somebody else rich and not live your own life. Chris decided he'd had enough and was going full time. As it happens it's worked out, but he does work hard.

Chris agrees with him. "I probably work longer hours now as a property entrepreneur. You're constantly looking at deals, packaging and working on something to do with the business, but I don't mind that because I know where I'm going and what I'm trying to achieve."

He adds: "It's a collective bunch of situations which has made me glad I went into this, like family time. Last summer I was able to take my boy to the beach on a Wednesday afternoon and I can say, what are you doing today? I can play with you in the park. It's those things I'm thankful for. Property has given me space and time, and the financial freedom that comes with that. Now it's a case of making sure I keep going. That's where my goal is, to go higher and higher."

Samuel says: "Chris has faced some tough challenges, but he has come through them by knowing the market and the price point. Now he's moving on to bigger sourcing deals and developments. That's the transition I recommend people to do.

"He's an asset to the academy. Everyone wants to pick his brain because he's achieved so much. He's working with some pretty high net worth individuals looking to do business with him, and my property team are very interested in what he's doing. He's a fabulous guy who deserves his success. He's got some exciting projects lined up with potentially massive returns. I'm sure there is a lot more to come from him yet."

CHRIS' TIPS

"Set yourself realistic goals, to start with, and then something that will take a long time to achieve but it's a dream. For me I wanted to become financially free and quit my job. There are so many strategies you can do. I narrowed it down to rent-to-rent, understood the ins and outs and took action."

"Look at yourself and find what you want. Where do you want to be in five years? Do you want to be in the same job or be your own boss? Start finding out what that passion is. Get the knowledge and act."

"One of things that incentivised me is you don't need to go to university to become a qualified professional investor. It's about taking action and learning along the way. There's so much information out there. Learn it and then implement it."

"People look at property and try to get the quick buck but to me it's a long game. It's all about the relationships you build."

Chapter 26 – Errol 'DJ Paleface' Reid

Songwriter ploughs royalties from global hit into property after studying Samuel Leeds' videos

Celebrities and sport stars frequently turn to Property Investors' founder Samuel Leeds for advice on how to invest their money in the housing market. One of those personalities is Errol 'DJ Paleface' Reid who wrote the chorus to Drake's huge international hit *One Dance*.

Errol 'binge-watched' Samuel's videos for two years to learn about different strategies and then built up a portfolio of buy-to-lets using the proceeds from the single. Now Samuel is supporting him with the next step on his entrepreneurial journey as he considers moving into property developing.

The two men met up when the musician agreed to appear on *Winners on a Wednesday* as a thank you to his mentor for helping him get started in property investing. As someone who has Asperger's and suffers from social anxiety, Errol does not usually give interviews. However, he was keen to share his experience and endorse Samuel's training.

During his chat with Samuel the songwriter explained how he had to get his wife Kyla to understand property before he could start investing in it. She does not involve herself in business, but they always make decisions together. So, he knew he had to win her over first.

"I said to her there's no point in me just doing this and you not understanding what's going on. I knew she wasn't going to read the property books, so I said to her one night, look at this video. This geezer's going to shout at you but at the end of it you'll get it. Everything [about property] I've been trying to tell you he summarises.

"At the end she said, he's good Errol, I get it."

The 'geezer' was Samuel who received a message afterwards from Errol, encouraging him to keep on producing the videos because they 'worked' and to ignore any haters he might get. Errol says the free content on YouTube provides a hugely valuable source of information without having to trawl through 'a massive book' to find it.

"For example, on HMO licensing, you're going to find contradictory information simply because the rules vary from one area to another, depending on the council. Samuel comes on and tells you exactly what to do. It's just concise. Those videos helped me to get my missus on board to start investing in property."

Errol and Kyla opted to purchase three to four-bedroom properties for between £160,000 and £180,000 and rent them out as affordable housing to workers.

Getting onto the property ladder, however, proved to be harder than they anticipated. *One Dance* is one of the best-performing singles of all time. It broke a world record in 2016 for more than one billion streams on Spotify and also topped the charts in 15 countries including the UK, USA and Canada. And yet, despite this phenomenal success, Errol and his singer-wife Kyla, who features as a guest vocalist on the song, were twice declined a mortgage as they attempted to get a foothold in the private rented sector.

Errol has earned a lot of money as a producer of house and garage music – his catalogue of songs was recently valued at £1.2m. But due to the way the music industry works, songwriters have to wait for their royalties to come in, he explains.

"The Performing Rights Society is my lifeline. If you write a song, you don't even have to perform it. You can write the song down and the lyrics and give it to someone. Every time it gets played on radio or TV or broadcast in a shop, that shop [or station] has to pay a PRS licence fee."

The PRS collects the fees and then distributes them in the form of royalties to members whose music has been used. Yet, it can take several months for the payments to be made.

"Say *One Dance* gets played on the radio today, you've got to wait at least six months for the PRS to hit and come back round," says Errol who owns the Northern Line Records label.

The Society also pays out royalties on other uses of music on streaming services such as Spotify, which again take several months to filter through the system. This directly affected his mortgageability – just as the couple were trying to buy their first house.

Initially, they wanted to put down a deposit of £100,000 and obtain a mortgage of £200,000. As they were self-employed, the bank demanded to see all their accounts including evidence of their earnings for the past four years.

"They also wanted a letter from the accountant saying we were going to be capable of earning a certain amount of money. We jumped through all these hoops but then we were told we'd been declined a mortgage," Errol recalls.

By this time three months had gone by, and they had raised another £100,000. So, this time they applied to borrow £100,000 but their application was again turned down. Instead they decided to buy the house with cash. They also paid the Stamp Duty and bought their first buy-to-let outright after saving a further £100,000.

Since then they have acquired three more buy-to-lets and are hoping to expand their portfolio as *One Dance* and other music continues to be a money-spinner for them.

Errol was training to be a train driver to gain some security when the opportunity came along to collaborate with the Canadian rapper Drake. It was to become a life-changing event for both him and his wife. He watched the track climb up the US charts in amazement as it overtook another single released by Drake on the same day featuring Kayne West and Jay-Z.

One Dance, which also features Nigerian singer Wizkid, became the best-performing single worldwide of 2016 and remained number one in the UK charts for 15 consecutive weeks.

"It still doesn't feel real," says Errol who is the entrepreneur out of the two of them.

All the buy-to-lets they have bought so far have been in the area where Kyla grew up which has given Errol a good understanding of local house prices and how much to pay. Not all his dealings, though, have gone smoothly. In fact, his first purchase of a leasehold property fell through two weeks before the completion when the seller pulled out. His wife was annoyed at losing £1,000 in solicitor's fees, so Errol promised her he would find a better property for them to buy. True to his word, he tracked down a rare opportunity to acquire a one-bedroom house. It was on the market for £15,000 more than the other one but it was being offered freehold and was in a perfect spot on a high street. That sale went ahead and is now working well as an investment.

Errol says he is 'harsh' when it comes to negotiating. It also helps that he thinks logically and is not emotion-based in his decision making. His guiding principle is that sellers usually put their homes on the market at inflated prices to achieve their target of what they will accept.

"The last house we saw was on for £180,000 but wasn't worth a penny more than £165,000. I told the estate agent I'll make an offer but tell the owner if he doesn't accept it then my next offer is going to be £10,000 lower.

"If you want to be greedy and hold out for someone else to come along then OK, but I'm not waiting around because at the moment I've got that money set aside. It's potentially going to take a minimum of two months on average to complete the house sale. It can even be up to five months, especially at the moment.

"Cash is king in property. If you're a cash buyer, you negotiate because that's the way the whole market is set up."

These days Errol and Kyla can demonstrate that they have enjoyed a high income for the past three years which makes raising finance for property investing far easier.

"I'm about to do a royalty financing deal at the moment so that I can free up some funds to invest in more buy-to-lets," says Errol. "It also has the advantage that any interest you pay is tax-deductible."

He regards property as a far better investment than stocks and shares, which are volatile and require research, or even gold.

"I bought a couple of gold bullion coins because there is no UK Capital Gains Tax (due to it being legal tender). It's a good way of saving money but not a good way of making money.

"Property is the only thing where in my opinion if I put £50,000 down now then in five years' time that £50,000 is still there but it's made me £7,000 a year [in rent]. And it's a passive income, barring the roof coming down or leaking. There's not really much you have to do if you get a decent estate agent to manage it."

Errol is a fan of Samuel's content, but he also admires him for the way he disproved the billionaire magnet Lord Alan Sugar's claims that he had never given Samuel business advice. That was another reason for coming on his show.

"Samuel has helped me with what I'm doing, and he's helped a lot of other people I know, including my friend T2 (who produced the hit single *Heartbroken).* He told me he's been to one of Samuel's crash courses and was on point. I feel honoured to speak on the show about property."

Samuel says: "It's great that people like Errol are not only investing in property but speaking out about it. There are a lot of people in the music industry making very good money, but they don't know how to invest it.

"Errol got educated and put his PRS money into the private rented sector which gives you a stable income. That then makes you more mortgageable and it has enabled him to get better leverage on his finance. Now he still has that money coming in, which is unlikely to stop, but he's also got the capital appreciation from his properties and cash flow. So, he's in a good place."

He adds: "A lot of rich or successful people hide away so they don't get haters or people asking them for money. I appreciate Errol sharing his story and I'm sure he'll inspire a lot of other people. I'll be helping him out taking on bigger things in development."

ERROL'S TIPS

"Find a good estate agent who you have an honest relationship with because estate agents can pressurise you into buying things that are not good."

"Find a decent solicitor who specialises in property investment. It will save you a lot of time and headaches. We hear nothing from our solicitors until the day before completion. They sort out any issues before that."

"Unless you're buying a house for yourself, don't rush out and buy the first property you see. Wait for the property to be on the market for six months."

"Don't put all your eggs in one basket. If you get a dip in one of your income streams, like you always do, that can't have a knock-on effect in the way you live your life."

"Try to surround yourself with positive people, rather than energy thieves who leave you feeling tired because they're constantly saying you can't do this or that."

"Watch Samuel's videos. Educate yourself with someone you can understand. Process the information and apply it."

Chapter 27 – Nigel Dube

Young Property Investors student cashes in on property despite losing £8,000 on his first deal

Many people of Nigel Dube's generation would give their eye teeth to be in his position. Still only in his early twenties, he is making more than £3,000 a month from rent-to-rent deals. Not only that, he already has a firm foot on the ladder to becoming a homeowner by the age of 30 – something a lot of his contemporaries could only dream of achieving in today's inflated housing market.

And yet Nigel's story is one of caution. He lost £8,000 on his first rent-to-rent transaction because he jumped in before he was fully prepared. It was thanks to his training with Property Investors that the graduate managed to recover and now has a mixed rental portfolio which includes lease option agreements – the 'golden ticket' for any investor.

Zimbabwe-born Nigel emigrated to England with his parents when he was 12. They came in search of work and opportunity, and, like them, he too has found it in his adopted country. After leaving school, Nigel moved from Luton to Birmingham to study mechanical engineering at university. At that point his future looked secure, but he felt dissatisfied.

"When I was at uni, I didn't really like the life. I always thought I wanted something different, something more," says Nigel looking back.

Reading Robert Kiyosaki's best-selling personal finance book *Rich Dad, Poor Dad,* which advocates investing in real estate, influenced him to change the direction of his life. While still at university, he took on a full-time job as a stock controller in a warehouse. His game plan was simple.

He wanted to save as much money as he could and put it into bricks and mortar to build wealth.

It soon became apparent that it would require hard graft if he was to realise his ambition.

"It was a decent job, but it was very intense," he explains. "There were 12-hour shifts sometimes."

In spite of the long hours, Nigel still found time to watch videos about property which was now uppermost in his thoughts. During his research he came across Samuel Leeds' YouTube channel after a recommendation from an American investor and was immediately hooked.

"It explored a whole new world, like rent-to-rents, and I began binge-watching Samuel's videos, but I was still at work, so even though I was getting all this knowledge, I wasn't doing anything about it."

With this in mind, Nigel paid for a VIP ticket to get a front-row seat at the Property Investors Crash Course in November 2018. It was money well spent, he says.

"It was a special moment for me. I wanted to get as much knowledge as I could. Samuel had inspired me so much before with his videos. I paid less than £100 for a course that lasted two days."

Feeling 'super-motivated' by all the strategies he had learnt about on the Property Investors Crash Course, he then enrolled on the *Deal Finding Extravaganza* course which was due to take place in the new year. However, in his eagerness to get started he went on some property viewings straight away.

Within days Nigel, who was still employed at the time, had negotiated his first rent-to-rent deal on a three-bedroom house in Smethwick, Birmingham. Under the agreement, he would pay the owner a guaranteed monthly rent and then let the rooms at a higher rate and keep the profit. As part of the arrangement, he also had to pay a deposit up front, covering the rent for the first three months.

His intention was to add another bedroom to increase his rental income and make it a viable proposition.

"It was open plan downstairs with a separate kitchen, so I thought I'd partition a wall [for the extra bedroom]."

But then the landlord objected. Having spent money on furnishing and decorating the house, Nigel found that he had just £2,000 of his savings left. Nigel admits it was a bad deal. Fortunately, he had a break clause which allowed him to pull out of it after six months.

"I felt terrible about losing so much money, but I knew it wasn't right to blame Samuel. I was waiting for training, which was coming, and I'd decided I just wanted to take action immediately.

"Especially after watching Samuel's video about his Financial Freedom Challenge, I remember I messaged him on Facebook and said I wanted to quit my job. Samuel said it was probably not the best idea before I actually got money coming in. But in my head, I was so super-crazy because he had opened my eyes to a whole different world of how you can get passive income."

Samuel says it highlights the dangers of not getting properly educated before investing in property. "It's great to take action but things can go wrong. I do think it's important to pay for training because you can make and lose money in the housing market.

"It's a dangerous place to be in when you're desperate for a deal. When you get trained and get lots of deals in front of you, it's a better place to come from."

Many investors would be put off by such a disastrous start to their property journey, but Nigel refused to give up. He reconnected with some of the people he had met at the crash course who gave him some advice. Then, armed with a stack of information from the *Deal Finding Extravaganza,* he decided to focus instead on the serviced accommodation sector.

Changing his strategy proved to be a clever move. Nigel negotiated another rent-to-rent deal this time with the landlord of a flat in Birmingham's tallest residential tower block, Brindley House in Newhall Street. Nigel agreed on a rental of £800 a month and then rented it out as furnished accommodation for short stay lets.

Within months it was giving him lucrative returns. "It fluctuated, depending on the time of year, but it was grossing £3,500 in August (2019). The average profit in a month was £1,200. It's not doing so well now because of the Covid-19 pandemic, but I've still got it."

More successes were to follow as he pursued different types of rent-to-rent arrangements. His portfolio now includes three rent-to-rent HMOs (house shares). Two are making a profit of £850 per month each, while the other one – a three-bed town house converted into an HMO – is generating a monthly return of £700.

The young entrepreneur has also clinched much sought-after lease option agreements on two flats – after being taught the strategy by Samuel. One of the options is with a landlord who lives in Canada.

Nigel was searching for a property which he could rent out to visitors when he came across a listing for an apartment in Coventry city centre. During the viewing the estate agent informed him that the owner would be willing to sell the flat if Nigel did not want to take it on as serviced accommodation.

As a fledgling investor, he could not believe his luck. He realised in a flash it was a massive opportunity but took time to collect his thoughts before responding.

"I was thinking, what does Samuel normally say in this situation?! I had to gather myself a bit and pretend I was still looking round but I was thinking what to say. Then I said what if I rent it and buy at the same time, but the completion would be in the next five years.

"The agent was open to the idea, but I was worried he wouldn't pitch it to the landlord as I would. So, I said, talk to him first but is it OK if I also talk to him afterwards. That was OK but when he pitched it to him, the guy called me straight away to ask a couple of questions."

Nigel explained the principle behind lease option agreements but was careful to follow Samuel's advice not to answer any legal questions. Instead he told the landlord to consult a solicitor on the ins and outs of the strategy.

As the property was tired and had been on the market for a couple of months, he made an offer of £175,000 - £20,000 below the asking price –

with the option to buy the property in five years' time and no deposit to pay. He was delighted when the owner agreed to his terms.

After finding a solicitor through Facebook, Nigel picked up the keys within a month of the viewing in October 2019.

Having done up the apartment, it is now generating a profit for him, despite the coronavirus lockdowns which have hit many investors hard in the pocket. His margin in November 2020, during the second lockdown, amounted to £250. This was after paying the owner £800, which includes the mortgage, ground rent and service fee.

The accommodation is advertised through booking.com and Airbnb. Once the restrictions on travel are lifted and tourism picks up, he expects the monthly yield to rise significantly.

The benefit of a lease option agreement like this one is clear, says Samuel. "Hopefully in five years the apartment will be worth a lot more. Then Nigel can exercise the option at £175,000 and he's got the profit and the capital appreciation. Basically, he's benefiting from the property as if he owned it. He's getting the growth and the cash flow but didn't pay a deposit. That's a good deal."

Not all deals are a good as that, though. Nigel returned the keys to another property which he had negotiated on a lease option because it was not working.

Samuel approves of weeding out the bad ones. "You are going to have properties that over-perform and under-perform. The important thing is to get rid of the ones that under-perform and keep filling your pipeline with ones that are going to over-perform."

Nigel's next property has the potential to give him excellent returns. He has secured a rent-to-rent agreement with the landlord of a four-bedroom house in Birmingham which he plans to turn into a six-bed HMO. The owner has already applied for a licence. Once that comes through, the conversion work can begin, and Nigel will start looking for tenants.

His profits from property now add up to around £3,200 a month, the equivalent of a respectable salary in the UK. Even with the challenges of Covid, he remains hungry to land more deals. When the serviced accommodation side of his business slumped following the outbreak, he watched Samuel's videos again to refresh his knowledge. He also joined Samuel 365, Property Investors' online training programme, which offers weekly coaching webinars with Samuel, as well as unlimited one-to-one support, access to courses and other benefits.

Nigel says the courses are good value for money when compared to his student loan of nearly £30,000. "It costs £95 a month and you can try it out for seven days for £1 which is crazy.

"I'm gaining as much information as I can from there so that I can increase my cash flow by doing at least another 10 deals in the next 12 months."

Samuel says: "What I like about Nigel is that he is constantly transitioning. He's completed different rent-to-rent deals and then moved onto lease option agreements. Now he's looking at doing buy, refurbish and refinance projects, as well as deal sourcing.

"He's done amazingly well, and the mad thing is he's just getting started. Who can say at his age I've got lease option agreements, rent-to-rents and I've had to hustle from scratch with no prior property experience? Nigel has gone through the training with Samuel 365. One day he's going to be a mentor and an inspiration to many people. I'm ridiculously proud of him."

NIGEL'S TIPS:

"I negotiated another lease option agreement but gave the keys back because it wasn't working. As Samuel says, you should get rid of under-performing properties and just concentrate on the ones that are going to over-perform."

"It's important to pay for training to avoid losing money like I did. I was so motivated after the Property Investors Crash Course to go out and get a deal but it's best to get a few options in front of you before making a decision."

"Connect with other investors. I have and it's helped me. I posted messages on Facebook groups to find my solicitor."

"Check the head lease when you're about to complete a rent-to-rent deal on serviced accommodation to make sure there are no restrictions on sub-letting it."

Chapter 28 – Ricci Mandal

Ex-DJ who left school with no qualifications turns his life around through property

Former DJ Ricci Mandal went into property so that he could make his family proud of him after being kicked out of school with no GCSEs. Ricci achieved that aim and much more, thanks to his training with Property Investors. He went into business with his parents and two sisters, making money out of rent-to-serviced accommodation, and in three months became financially free.

Not content to stop there, he has progressed to providing a deal sourcing service, while still making a fortune out of renting out furnished rooms for short stays.

His family have another reason to be impressed with him. Before the Covid crisis, Ricci regularly appeared on stage at Property Investors' events to talk about his success and to pass on tips. In fact, the 28-year-old sees it as his mission to pass on his knowledge to others and help them become financially independent through property.

Ricci and Samuel Leeds have that in common. Both men believe passionately in the power of education to transform people's lives for the better. And Samuel often trusts Ricci to explain the rent-to-serviced accommodation strategy to new students.

They are firm friends too. Their relationship, however, got off to a rocky start, as far as Ricci was concerned. Taking up the story, he says:

"I knew property was going to outlast me and I knew DJ-ing was just trading my time for money. My sister went to one of the free Property

Investors Crash Courses and she said it was the best place for beginners because you learn the basics.

"So, I messaged Samuel on Facebook and asked when the crash course was coming to Belfast. I was living in Northern Ireland at the time. Samuel didn't say hello. He just said get to the next one.

"To be honest, at first I did think this guy's an idiot and I won't bother messaging him again. But after a while I thought he's successful. He's where I want to be, so I need to listen to what he says and just do it. I booked on the course literally five minutes later."

Ricci sent Samuel a screenshot of the booking and said: "I'm in," to which Samuel replied: "Good man."

They laugh now when they remember their online exchange.

"I actually called him Rocco as well! says Samuel. "At the time people were always messaging me asking me when I was coming to their town.

"People would fly from all over the world to be at the crash course. If you're stopped by a two-hour plane journey or, in Ricci's case, a short boat ride, then you're stoppable. You have to make that effort."

Ricci also booked his sister Kiri and father Raj onto the crash course and shortly afterwards moved back to England. It was June 2018, when they attended the event. Ricci was still doing some DJ-ing but looking for work.

At the crash course, he soon found himself out of his comfort zone because of the motivational music which was being played.

"I sat at the back with my arms folded, thinking I don't want to be here anymore. I'm the DJ. I don't clap. I don't create energy. I just play the music. I'm the cool guy."

Looking back, Ricci understands that the music is part of keeping would-be property entrepreneurs awake during the two long days of training. It also creates an atmosphere conducive to audience participation which includes calling agents and role-playing.

The free crash course proved invaluable, despite Ricci's initial reluctance to get involved. He learnt how to work out the return on investment on a property and how to find deals. It was the stepping-stone to joining the Property Investors Academy with his family.

Ricci was keen to get going and before starting on the academy he began ringing agents to try to get a rent-to-serviced accommodation deal. He was dedicated to his task, making calls every day, but never succeeding.

"I was making mistake after mistake, saying the wrong things. I didn't quite understand the legalities behind rent-to-SAs, like head leases and mortgages. I was a bit like a headless chicken."

In total, he made 162 calls without landing a single deal. All that changed when the fledgling entrepreneur attended the Rent-to-Rent Revolution course on the academy.

"I remember saying to Samuel I've made all these calls. What am I doing wrong? I was saying things like, do you do serviced accommodation? The agents were just saying we don't do that and putting the phone down.

"I'd read *Go for No!* which says that you should go for as many no's as you can because the more no's you get the closer you are to a yes, and that's what motivated me."

Samuel believes there are two reasons why people fail. They either refuse to take action or they take massive action but lack the training to do it properly.

"You've got to be persistent. But the problem is that if you're just going for no, without the skill you'll have a trillion no's unless you get lucky. Ricci developed a thick skin, but his approach was wrong. He was saying, I'm doing corporate lets on a rent-to-rent basis. Is that something you would consider? That's wrong."

Samuel scrapped what Ricci was saying and got him to do a role-playing exercise where he was himself and Samuel was the agent. This is the script Ricci now uses, based on how their conversation went and what he was taught to say:

"Hi, my name's Ricci. I just saw one of your apartments online – a two-bedroom one on Samuel Road. Is that still available?

Samuel: Yes, it is.

Ricci: I was just wanting to ask a few questions about it, if that's OK.

Samuel: Absolutely. What would you like to know?

Ricci: Cool. The pictures look good. It's in good condition. Is the landlord looking for a long-term or short-term let?

Samuel: The landlord is looking for a long-term let.

Ricci: OK. Perfect. I'm looking to take on apartments like this for long-term lets. What I'm going to be doing is putting my own clients in there on short lets and letting them stay. I will take care of any maintenance and any void periods and I'm going to guarantee you the rent. Is this something you guys would be interested in?

Samuel: I can speak to the landlord and see if he would be interested. So, you're a company, right?

Ricci: I'm a company. It would be on a corporate let.

Samuel: What's the name of your company?

Ricci: It's called MP Sourced.

Samuel: I'll speak to the landlord and check out your company and give you a call back.

Ricci: Yes sure. In fact, I'll give you a call back. Is it OK if I call you back tomorrow at two o'clock or Wednesday at four o'clock?

Samuel: I think the landlord might be away. Give me till Wednesday and I'll try to speak to him. But if I do hear back, I'll give you a call back on this number.

Ricci: I'll speak to you then. Cheers.

Samuel: Bye."

Ricci used this new way of introducing himself in a real-life situation during the course and immediately hooked himself a rent-to-SA agreement on a luxury, one-bed furnished apartment within The Hub development in Milton Keynes – a 'city in a city' with a water fountain and public plaza surrounded by bars and restaurants.

"It worked because I was being transparent. I let them know what I was going to be doing from the off, but I was also telling them the value I was going to bring to them."

He also found a two-bed apartment in the same block. "We got the second flat the same day. The agent rang straight after the first one saying the landlord was willing to accept a corporate let. I viewed both with dad and we paid £300 to secure the second one."

Prior to the pandemic each one was making an average profit of £1,000 per month.

Explaining the strategy, Ricci says: "Rent-to-serviced accommodation is where you rent a property from a landlord. Then you rent it out yourself on short lets through sites like Airbnb and booking.com or you have corporate clients staying there on a short-term basis. It could be for a few days or a few weeks.

"In some areas serviced accommodation is more in demand than other places. It works in every big popular town and city."

Asked what gets him up in the morning, he replies: "Just knowing I can go out there and spend time on things I want to spend time on. I also want to build a legacy for my future family and the family I have now. Building a business with people I love gives me a buzz.

"And I love being around Samuel and other people who have come through the Property Investors Academy, like Alasdair Cunningham and Anthony Wilmott – and all the other academy members I meet."

Having a support network has been vital to his success as a property entrepreneur. "You keep on pushing through when you're in an environment where you can ask for help if you have a problem."

Ricci became financially free through his rent-to-SA dealings. But packaging and selling deals to investors has become an equally important part of his strategy to create a healthy cash flow. He stopped being a DJ less than a year after going on the crash course and became a compliant sourcer. For each deal he finds and negotiates he charges a commission of around £2,500. He has sourced all kinds of lucrative opportunities, from rent-to-rents to development deals. They included two in The Hub which netted him £5,000 early on in his career as an entrepreneur.

Technically, Ricci could take his foot off the accelerator and retire while still only in his twenties, but he loves the property game too much to take a step back just yet. The key to staying focused, he believes, is to set a goal and then, when you hit that, to set another one.

"You need to know where you want to be in one, two, three years' time or even five years' time. When I became financially free, I knew what my mission was and why I was doing it. Your mission and your why may change a little bit but you need to know what your next goal is.

"Every day you need to wake up and think what's my mission? If you get comfortable, you'll stay in that place. It's hard then to move forward. I wanted to give back and still do. That's why I came back to all the crash courses.

"When I started, I didn't know a thing. Everyone was so helpful. Samuel was helpful. I want to go back and say I was in your position once, now I'm here to help you as much as I can and answer any questions. I can't do that without staying relevant in property."

Ricci attended 10 Property Investors Crash Courses in four months during 2019 and is eager to get back on stage when the live events return.

He draws his strength from his guru. "Every time I'm around Samuel I'm inspired. If I'm feeling down, I'll get lifted up. He's just completely different to everyone else. He's motivating and just a genuinely nice, down-to-earth guy."

The feeling is mutual. Property Investors' founder says: "Before Ricci came on the crash course, he was looking for jobs, but couldn't get any because he had no qualifications. He had the drive and hunger, though, to do well. Now he's uber successful through rent-to-rents and a successful sourcing company as well which is making a lot of profit.

"I'm overwhelmed by his progress, not only in property but also as an influencer. Sometimes when I'm running an event or I'm at a crash course and it gets to the session where I'm supposed to talk about serviced accommodation, I think Ricci could probably explain this better than me. When he goes on stage, or speaks at one of our courses, like the *Deal Finding Extravaganza*, he gets such great positive feedback. That's my compliment to him."

RICCI'S TIPS

These are my five tips if you want to become an excellent deal sourcer:

- Maintain a good reputation. Always give refunds if you need to and never give out bad deals.

- Be consistent. If you say you're going to send out deals every week, do it.

- Be compliant. Don't break the rules. Make sure you stay legal.

- Always give lots of value. The best way to get investors and people to like and trust you is to give value.

- Do everything yourself while you're building your business. Go on viewings and networking events. Make sure you do it all first yourself, so you're learning along the way and you've got trust in your deals.

Chapter 29 – James Armstrong

Academy student who got off to a flying start and is still on cloud nine

In March 2019, James Armstrong sold a portfolio of 16 houses to an investor. His fee was three per cent of the purchase price. Give or take, that amounted to a cool £65,000. He shared the eye-watering commission with a Property Investors Academy student who had passed on the deal to him to sell.

At the time James was just 21 and had only been in property a couple of years, having trained on the academy himself. He reinvested all of the money in bricks and mortar and has never looked back since.

The former electrician was chosen to compete in *The Eviction 2019* and then teamed up with the winner, Anthony Wilmott. Together, they made more than £200,000 in six months from finding lucrative investment opportunities in the housing market.

James continues to make thousands of pounds a month from deal sourcing and is engaged in numerous joint venture projects, including the construction of a housing estate and a conversion of a disused pub into luxury apartments.

In 2020, James and Anthony raised more than £1m in investor finance and are working together on other major development deals. He has also linked up with Anthony and another investor to convert a beautifully located Welsh castle, Plas Gwynfryn, into stylish apartments. They are determined to bring the castle back from the ashes after it was wrecked by fire forty years ago, leaving it with no windows, doors or floors.

James says he lives mainly off rents from his properties and profits from 'flips,' all of which have made him financially independent. But while he likes the good things in life, the money is not his focus.

"It's nice, don't get me wrong, but it's not what I enjoy. I enjoy doing the deals and being around successful people."

That was key to him on his journey to becoming a property entrepreneur. James became a compliant deal sourcer after meeting Samuel Leeds at a Christian business networking group.

"At the time I was looking to go self-employed. I wasn't in control of the hours I worked, when I could go on holiday or how much I got paid. I thought I deserved more.

"When I listened to Samuel talking about property it sounded awesome. He gave me a copy of his book about how anyone can become financially free in a short time through investing in property."
After attending the free, two-day Property Investors Crash Course, he became a member of the company's academy in June 2018. Two months later he gave up his job after the money started rolling in from his bespoke sourcing business. It was initially called Acquérir from the French word for acquire and has since been rebranded as AWT Sourcing.

Like anyone in life who achieves their dreams, there are always hurdles to overcome. James, who was still living at home when he went into business, had to have the courage of his convictions to get started.

"My parents were never against me. They weren't a drag on my journey, but they've never supported me financially. They've supported me emotionally by getting behind me and they're always encouraging me to do more. So that's invaluable but I wasn't born with a silver spoon up my a**se.

"I didn't come from an investing background with assets behind me. I built this from the ground up with £200."

When he joined the Property Investors Academy and enrolled on the *Deal Finding Extravaganza*, he got into debt to the tune of £15,000 to pay for the training.

"Some people did have something to say about that, but at the time I'd already taken the loan out so what were they going to do? People who know me know I'm just going to do it anyway. I will listen to you but whatever I want to do I'm just going to do it anyway. They knew that and said just make it work. We may as well encourage you rather than try to undermine you and say that was a stupid decision."

Having absorbed all the training he could, he set off on the road to source deals, with an initial goal of making £2,000 a month so that he could give up his job. He soon doubled that figure and then trebled it later when he collaborated with Anthony.

Bagging a hefty commission early on from the sale of the 16-house portfolio gave him a huge lift. It consisted of six guesthouses, six house shares and four single lets, with a purchase price of around £2.3m and a rental income of £500,000 a year. By chance another member of the Property Investors Academy had got chatting to the owner who no longer wanted to manage them and was selling them as a job lot. The student had only recently begun deal sourcing and had not yet got a list of investors to whom he could offer it. So, he passed the deal to James. He found a buyer from his list which he had built mainly through networking and Facebook.

Keeping the momentum going after such a good start was a challenge James had to overcome early on.

"I was so hyped up after the training. So, I had that initial motivation, but after that it begins to settle. When you get up in the morning, there's no one there. Samuel's not there shouting in your ear, saying go on, go do the deal.

"You have to begin to callus your mind and motivate yourself to do things every day. It's not necessarily a battle but you choose to make it a battle and to power through, just to get everything done.

"In the first few months the biggest challenge was to keep going. If you're in a tight spot where you've got to raise finance very quickly – Samuel's castle is a prime example – you know you just have to knuckle down for a few hours and make it happen. That's as simple as it is."

James' can-do attitude has won him plenty of plaudits, with investors from home and abroad clamouring for his services. Several have paid him retainers worth several hundred pounds a month to get priority access to the opportunities he finds through networking and trawling property sites such as Rightmove and Gumtree.

"Basically, I sit down with an investor and find out what the best investment is for them and how they can get the highest returns on their money. I vet them before I put them on my list because I need to know they are serious about investing before I spend time with them."

As well as scouring property websites, he goes networking across the country in the hunt for deals which will yield high returns on investment.

After identifying a target, he then researches house prices and rents in the local area, views the property, negotiates the price and puts together a package outlining the financial benefits. He also goes one step further by arranging the conveyancing and any refurbishment work required.

His attitude is one of practicality rather than emotion when it comes to judging a good deal.

"The ideal investor has around £200,000 in the bank. They want to buy more than one house and buy it quickly. More importantly, they don't want to view it. They're not fussed about photos, the condition or location. It's will it rent? Yes. How much will it rent for? What's my cash flow? How much money do I need to put into it? What's the return on investment? You could hand them a £2m sourcing fee. If the numbers worked out, they'd pay it."

To the perennial question of why he does not buy the deals he finds himself, his reply is simple.

"I probably need about £1m a month to buy every deal that comes through. I haven't got that money. Buying a house takes time. I couldn't buy lots of houses at once. I don't have time to do all of it."

And if someone asks him why they should pay a sourcing fee if they could have found the deal themselves, he has another quick-fire response. "I would say why haven't you found it?"

There is the added advantage that he is on the ground. Not everyone who wants to invest in the UK housing market is based here. One of his investors was from Dubai. Faced with a seven-hour flight to get to Britain and the cost of travel, it was well worth it to pay someone to do the research for him.

Before the Covid pandemic of 2020/21, James made a point of going to networking events and conferences in London, as well as Property Investors' Crash Courses to link up with potential foreign investors who had flown in from abroad. At the same time James was also benefiting from the education on offer.

"I got one client who had £3-4m in the bank and wanted to work exclusively with me. I also get a lot of repeat business. I tell the world I'm a property investor and that I work with foreign investors."

These days James has begun buying properties himself. He entered into a joint venture with another contestant from *The Eviction* to take on two buy, refurbish, refinance schemes. He has also co-authored a book with Samuel, entitled *A Guide to Making Property Compliance Easy!*

The Eviction moved him on in so many ways, he says. "It was so good, regardless of the winner's prize of £20,000. The most value that any contestant gets from it is what you learn about yourself and how putting yourself in those positions makes you feel when you're doing the different strategy challenges.

"When I went into the competition, I hadn't felt truly out of my comfort zone for a while, and I wanted to be because that's how you grow as a person. I was very much put outside my comfort zone and I loved it. I thrived off it."

James is a serial fan of Samuel Leeds' training, booking himself onto any new training programme that gets announced. It is another opportunity to find a new JV partner and learn something new.

"I live such a different life now. When I was still working as a sparkie and learning about property, I was working upwards of 60 hours a week. Now I work in two to three-hour stints every day and take a couple of hours for lunch.

"I play hockey whenever I can. I'm also a big fan of skiing and steak, and neither of those are cheap!"

He adds: "These days I don't run the business all that much as it's almost entirely systemised. We are taking on one development deal a month and we've done another seven figures in cap raises so far in 2021.

"Life is busy again but it is super-enjoyable. Being an entrepreneur really gives you a different outlook on the world, where you see opportunities every day. It's incredibly good for your mental health when every day is an opportunity to learn and grow - where people bring you things all the time and you just have the task of deciding what it is you want to do next."

Samuel says James has been one of his biggest success stories.

"He has done phenomenally well, especially when you consider how young he is. His life today is light years away from his old job as an electrician. He's been a great asset to the academy and I'm really proud of him."

JAMES' TIPS

"For someone starting out with little money and no previous experience of property, I'd say the first step is to book on the crash course.

"Absorb as much information as you can around property and investing, and around the mindset of the successful. You'll get the skills through the crash course and academy. You'll get your toolbox. But if you don't know how to use the tools in it and how to continually do that on a daily basis, that's when you're going to come unstuck.

"It's the mindset of the rich that is so powerful. Begin to learn that. The easiest way to do that is to surround yourself with wealthy people and you'll just pick it up or watch podcasts and read books on it."

Chapter 30 – Tony Crook

American entrepreneur, who started in property before Samuel Leeds was born, adopts his ways of investing

American millionaire businessman Tony Crook has been investing in property for decades, buying and doing up houses to increase their value and then selling or renting them out. It is a time-honoured method of making money in the housing market and he would have continued with this strategy, had he not met Samuel Leeds.

Tony purchased his first house shortly after emigrating to England in 1983 – before Samuel was even born. But it was the Property Investors founder who taught him about creative ways of generating profits from bricks and mortar, without even necessarily having to be the owner.

Now the 56-year-old is enjoying a fresh lease of life as a property entrepreneur by drawing on his new-found knowledge to expand his portfolio. He is also imparting his business expertise to Property Investors Academy students, coaching them in the essential skills needed to run a company.

Tony attended a Property Investors Crash Course after being employed by Samuel to teach his academy members about staff management, business plans and goal setting. It quickly dawned on Tony that he could learn a lot himself about property – even though he had been an investor for many years – and so he decided to join the academy himself.

Now, after completing the training, he is about to buy a 10-bed HMO in Lincoln and has also recently negotiated a rent-to-rent deal in Birmingham with some other students on the academy.

He is candid when he says that he had never heard of either strategy before coming to the Property Investors Crash Course.

"I'd done a few buy and refurbish projects, but I didn't know about any of the other strategies, like rent-to-rent and lease option agreements. I didn't even know what an HMO was before I met Samuel. The crash course was mind-blowing."

The principle behind rent-to-rents particularly fascinated him because as an investor you could use other people's money to make money.

"With investing in property, sooner or later you may run out of money. Rent-to-rent is a great strategy because you can keep on increasing your cash flow, so I was really interested in doing that."

Tony was also inspired by the training itself to go out and try new techniques of profiting from property.

"I've always found property exciting and interesting. When I went to the crash course, it opened my eyes and ears. I went on other mentors' courses, but they weren't quite the same.

"Samuel Leeds' training is infectious. It makes you get out there and do things. It's not just textbook training. I loved it on the crash course when Samuel said, 'I'm going to phone an estate agent now,' and he did it live in front of about 1,000 people. That showed me that it's not just textbook – this is how you do it. That's the big difference in the Samuel Leeds training I find."

Samuel is also grateful for the help Tony has given him since they first met through Doug D'Aubrey, Samuel's business mentor since the age of 17. Doug also happens to be Tony's cousin and he enlisted him as a professional business coach for his consultancy firm which is how the connection came about.

Tony served for three years in the US Navy before moving to this country and settling in North London. He went on to set up a successful printing firm and other businesses which have enabled him to indulge his passion for property.

"I started in business at a very young age," he explains. "I enjoyed working for myself. I understood how to leverage other people and other ways of making money through business. It came naturally to me. I was good at it and I still am good at it.

"I've run businesses for over 30 years now and my businesses have made over £100m of turnover in those years. Not only that, I've employed over 100 people in my time in business – people who have been with me for a long time. They've got partners and have bought houses and had children all under my watch. That makes me feel really good."

For the father-of-three business has always been his driving force, while property was a 'pleasure thing,' although now he is a lot wiser, he says.

His family lent him the money to acquire his first property when he was 20. At the time house prices were rising every month and he made around £40,000 when he subsequently sold it. After repaying his loan, it left him a chunk of money to go travelling around the world for two years.

On his return, he bought a house for £90,000 when prices had hit a high, hoping to see it go up in value again and then sell it on. Instead the market crashed and within six months his house was worth £55,000. A lot of homeowners handed the keys back to their mortgage company, but Tony held his nerve and rented it out as a single let. Despite interest rates running at 23 per cent, it still made him money.

"It paid my mortgage and actually made me a small profit every month which was great. It was like an awakening – I thought wow. Eventually the house prices went up. I sold it 10 years later at £180,000, so I doubled my money."

Samuel says Tony's experience shows how the market does recover in time.

"Some people are scared to buy property. They worry that there will be a crash, but even if it happens, you hold onto it. It doesn't matter because ultimately it's going to bounce back up."

Tony's printing company prospered by transitioning to a 24-hour, seven-day-a-week operation to provide much faster turnarounds on orders than competitors were offering. By being proactive in business and working 'smart,' he thrived and has been able to put money aside for property.

"When I went on holiday with my family, I was the sort of person who said wouldn't it be lovely to have a house here, so we bought one. But then we thought there's no point having a house in a place where you don't see it, so we rented it out as holiday let. Any time we had voids between lets we would go and have a free holiday."

These days Tony is pursuing more inventive deals. The purchase price of the HMO in Lincoln is £240,000. After spending £60,000 on doing up the bedrooms, he expects to pull out most of his money by refinancing the house on a commercial valuation of £380,000 to £400,000.

"With a 10-bed HMO it has to be a commercial valuation because it is a business which has a turnover and makes a profit. By valuing it on a commercial basis, rather than bricks and mortar, the lenders will value it at a much higher rate because it is worth more in business. It's like me buying another print company. It is a bona fide business."

The rent-to-rent agreement in Birmingham came about as a result of two Property Investors Academy members inviting him to accompany them on some viewings over a weekend. Together they put forward an offer which was accepted.

In business you need someone to reach out to, Tony believes.

"It can be a lonely place at the top, so to have training and mentorship is really important. It's something I've learned over the years.

"When I was young, I didn't think I needed help. I just thought this is something I'm going to do myself. I'll work really hard and I'm savvy. I was wrong in that.

"The art of business is making quick decisions. If you've got nobody to soundboard off, or share ideas with, then how do you know it's the right decision? Even if they don't know exactly what your business is, verbalising it and talking to somebody helps you judge whether you're making the right decision or not.

"I lost a lot of money a few years back. I didn't have anybody to warn me about some of the pitfalls when I over-extended myself. I paid for it big time. Luckily, I had my properties which I could bounce back on and I was able to recover, but if I'd reached out earlier and set my business up slightly differently, I wouldn't have been in that trouble in the first place.

"That's why, when I learned that, I decided to dedicate my life to trying to help others and stop them from making mistakes."

He spends hours on Zoom calls talking to academy members and encouraging them. "I like helping other people and I like success. It doesn't have to be my success. To feed off other people's success is really fulfilling.

"Another great thing about Samuel Leeds's company is that it appeals to all people. It's not necessarily people from privileged backgrounds who make money through property. I love dealing and working with them and helping them at their certain levels and just moving them along that step further."

Samuel agrees that having someone you can turn to is vital in property and business.

"If you haven't got a mentor or a trainer, you'll end up getting advice anyway from maybe your wife or kids, or Dave down the pub, and they're going to give you terrible advice, so you may as well get advice from the right people.

"It's important to ask yourself who are the five people you're getting advice off? Are those people financially free? If not, maybe you need to find some different people."

He also makes the point that if you employ a mentor or a coach, you not only grow yourself personally, you can claim it as a business expense.

Summing up Tony's achievements and input into his company, Samuel says: "People's biggest fear in property is that it is going to crash or that interest rates are going to rocket. Tony had both of those things happen to him but still made money. His passive income from his properties also baled him out when his business money stopped.

"It's fabulous to have him on board with Property Investors too. The great thing about having people like Tony involved in coaching our students is that it gives them the best of the best. He's also helped me personally and in my business. I'm really grateful for that and I'm so glad to see him winning in property."

Tony is equally thankful to his trainer and is excited by the opportunities opening up in front of him. "If I'd known what I did about property 30 years ago it would have been a completely different world for me, but I have no regrets. I'm still very young now and I'm learning. I've got a big future ahead of me and I've now decided a major part of my life is going to be property."

He has already achieved one of his goals when he became a member of the Property Investors Academy which was to appear on *Winners on a Wednesday* – Samuel's popular YouTube series featuring successful students. Tony regularly watches the show and enjoys listening to other investors' stories. With more than 100 episodes so far recorded, he has plenty of viewing material to keep him occupied.

TONY'S TIPS

"I would say education is the main thing you need to be a successful property investor. You need to know what's available to you and then you can decide what's best for you. I didn't know HMOs existed or rent-to-rents. If I'd known that years ago, I'd been in a different position now. Go out there and get as much knowledge as you can and then follow a process that you know works."

"Have mentorship and coaching. Reach out and don't just stay in your shell."

"I believe in having multiple income streams and not just relying on one strategy. Pre-Covid one of my properties was mainly serviced accommodation which hit a cliff. If all my property had been in that situation then I would be struggling."

"The business should be your vehicle to financial freedom and passive income. I've always used my business to have that."

Final thoughts from Samuel Leeds

I hope you have enjoyed reading about the remarkable progress of the students featured in this book and have been inspired by their property journeys.

They had four vital things in common. They all...

1. **TOOK MASSIVE ACTION:** To be successful you have to take big steps while others just talk about it. Implementation and hard work are key to being an entrepreneur.

2. **HAD BELIEF:** You need to believe in yourself and in the process. You will manifest what you expect to happen. Show a little faith and don't listen to the doubters

3. **GOT CREATIVE:** Problems are easy to find, but winners find solutions not problems. When it seems everything is going wrong, you need to get super creative and never take 'no' for an answer.

4. **GAINED KNOWLEDGE:** Property is the second best investment you can make - the best is yourself. All of these people decided to get trained and attended my property investment training programmes. Once you have the knowledge nobody can ever take it from you.

If you embrace these four attributes, don't be surprised when you start getting crazy results and maybe one day you will feature in one of these volumes.

If you have enjoyed these short stories and want to learn how you can achieve similar success, you can get a free ticket to my Property Investors Crash Course. For more information visit:
www.property-investors.co.uk

Have you already become financially free from my strategies and teachings? I would love to hear from you on social media. Alternatively, simply email team@property-investors.co.uk

Warmest wishes,

Samuel Leeds

Printed in Great Britain
by Amazon

61100611R00119